National Park Service
U. S. Department of the Interior

San Juan Island
National Historical Park

Museum Management Plan

Cultural Resources
Pacific West Region
2010

San Juan Island

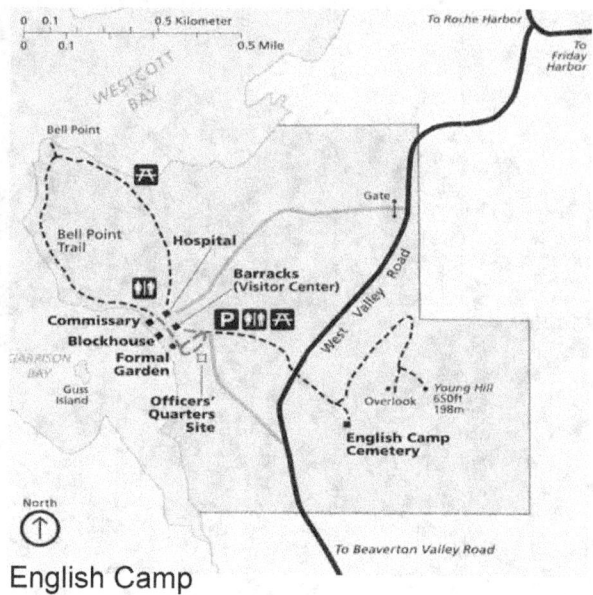

English Camp

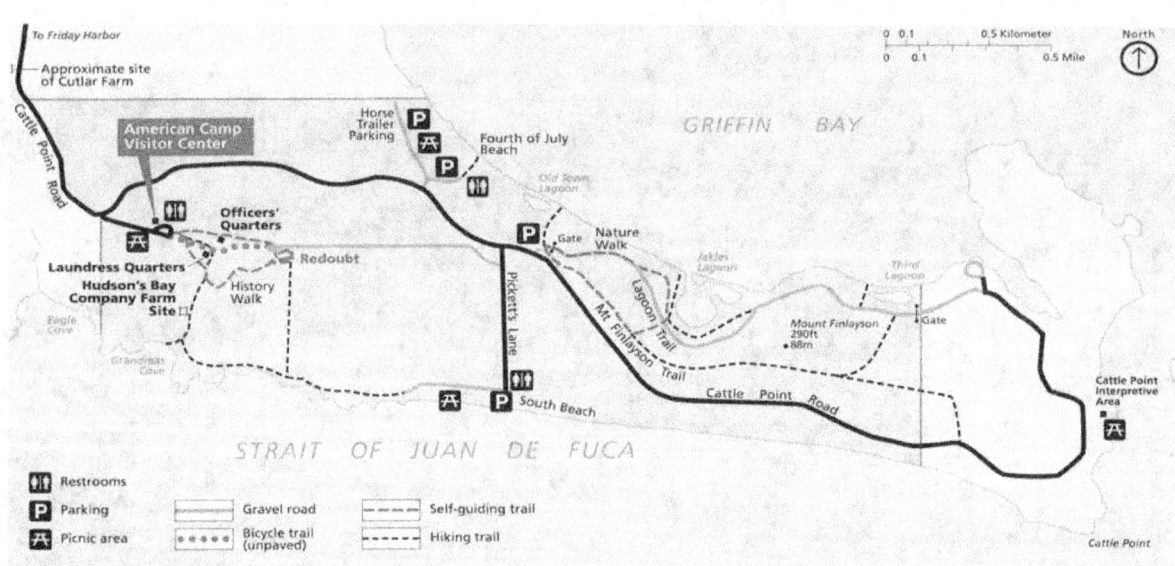

American Camp

San Juan Island National Historical Park

Museum Management Plan

Team Roster

Kelly Cahill, Curator
North Cascades National Park
Ebey's Landing National Historical Reserve
San Juan Island National Historical Park
Marblemount, Washington

Kirstie Haertel, Regional Archeologist
Pacific West Region
Seattle, Washington

Theresa Langford, Curator
Fort Vancouver National Historic Site
Vancouver, Washington

Diane Nicholson, Regional Curator
Pacific West Region
Oakland, California
(Team Leader)

Samantha Richert, Curator (SCEP)
Pacific West Region
Seattle, Washington

Paul Rogers, Archivist
Yosemite National Park
El Portal, California

Department of the Interior
National Park Service
Pacific West Region
2010

San Juan Island
National Historical Park

Museum Management Plan

Recommended By:

signature July 9, 2010

Diane L. Nicholson, Regional Curator   Date
Pacific West Region

Concurred By:

signature 7/16/2010

Peter Dederich, Superintendent   Date
San Juan Island National Historical Park

Approved By:

signature 7/29/10

George Turnbull, Acting, Regional Director   Date
Pacific West Region

Executive Summary

This Museum Management Plan (MMP) for the museum at San Juan Island National Historical Park (SAJH) identifies the key collection management issues facing the park, and presents a series of recommendations to address those issues. This plan was developed by a team of experienced museum collection management professionals working in cooperation with the park management team and staff.

The *North Cascades National Park Service Complex and Ebey's Landing National Historical Reserve Museum Management Plan* (2005) provides guidance on general collections management; programming, staffing, and budget. Therefore, this plan focuses on access, use, and research, as well as on the Marblemount Curation Facility, one of the locations where SAJH collections are located. Further actions in the North Coast and Cascades Network related to management changes at Fort Vancouver National Historic Site (FOVA) and the Vancouver National Historic Reserve have led to a proposal for the establishment of a curation repository for area parks to be located in a non-historic (1980s) building in that part of the Reserve to be transferred to the National Park Service in 2011. A portion of San Juan Island's collections are proposed to be included in that new facility.

Other collections (see Table 2) are currently located at Fort Vancouver National Historic Site and the Burke Museum of Natural History and Culture at University of Washington. The SAJH archeological collection is one of the most interesting and best documented archeological collections in the Pacific Northwest and those located at the Burke Museum are extensively used by researchers and students of museum studies and archeology.

The challenge, then, is to make these dispersed collections more accessible to and used by park staff and the public. This plan provides guidance on exploring non-traditional platforms and access points, such as using the Internet, social media, and other electronic means. The visibility of the museum collections could be increased by working with the partners currently housing those collections to expand their use, and by identifying additional partners, such as the San Juan Island Historical Museum, with which the park could develop more formalized agreements.

Key Recommendations

Several key recommendations are listed here, while additional and more detailed recommendations follow the discussion section of each issue in this plan.

- Develop and institute a park-level policy to plan for the orderly movement of park records into the park archives, which would maintain a permanent record of staff management and stewardship of park resources.

- Explore development of internet tools, including the use of the ICMS Web catalog, for making the museum collections accessible for research by park staff and the public.

- Update exhibits with more interpretive information about the artifacts.

- Formalize partnership agreements with the Burke Museum (for collections other than archeology).

- Develop programming requests for further interpretation, processing, research, and catalog updating for archeological collections.

- Work with the North Coast and Cascades Network Board of Directors to develop a broad-based museum management program that supports the needs of the parks in the network, including the development of a multi-park repository at FOVA, increasing the NOCA curator to full-time, and creating a network archivist position.

Table of Contents

List of Illustrations

List of Tables

Within the Pacific West Region, the Museum Management Plan (MMP) replaces the Collection Management Plan (CMP) referred to in National Park Service publications such as the *Outline for Planning Requirements; DO#28: Cultural Resource Management*; and the NPS *Museum Handbook*. Whereas the CMP process generally concentrates on the technical aspects of museum operations, the MMP recognizes that specific directions for these technical aspects already exist in the NPS *Museum Handbook* series.

The MMP process therefore does not duplicate that information. Instead it places museum operations in a holistic context within park operations by focusing on how collections may be used by park staff to support specific park goals. This plan recognizes that there are many different ways in which archives, libraries, and object collections may be organized, linked, and used within individual parks, and as a result provides park-specific advice on how this may be accomplished within this specific unit. Where necessary, material found in the NPS *Museum Handbook* or *Conserve-O-Gram* series will be referenced in the text, and where required, technical recommendations not covered will appear as appendices to this plan.

San Juan Island National Historic Park (SAJH) was established for the purpose of "…interpreting and preserving the sites of the American and English camps on the island, and of commemorating the historic events that occurred from 1853 to 1871 on the island in connection with the final settlement of the Oregon Territory boundary dispute, including the so-called Pig War of 1859." Created by Congress in 1966 (80 Stat. 737), it was preceded by National Historic Landmark status (1961) and land acquisition by the Washington State park system. The park was officially dedicated in 1972.

SAJH has a very small park staff and budget. In FY 2009, the adjusted base budget was $812,000 with 9.66 FTE. Since 1993, North Cascades National Park (NOCA) has housed and managed much of the SAJH collections. The NOCA curator (GS-1015-11) is the curator-of-record for SAJH; NOCA funds this position at .5 FTE. The remainder of her work year is supported through $13,000 of SAJH funds (about four pay periods); two pay periods from Ebey's

Landing National Historic Reserve (EBLA); and project funds or work at other parks. An annual agreement (see Appendix A) outlines what the NOCA curator will accomplish on the SAJH collection. SAJH has entered into additional agreements to manage discrete archeological collections; one is with the Burke Museum, University of Washington, for management of much of the pre-contact archeological collections (Appendix B), and the other is with Fort Vancouver National Historic Site (FOVA) for management of the historical archeological collections associated with Belle Vue Sheep Farm, a Hudson's Bay Company site. The NOCA and Burke agreements are current; however, the last agreement with FOVA dates from 1995. The 1998 agreement (Appendix C), while signed, was never implemented, according to the former FOVA curator.

The park collection is currently in excess of 900,000 items (see Table 1). The numbers change as archeological and archival collections are processed and cataloged, leading to more accurate numbers in the park's museum catalog database (ICMS). SAJH museum collections are primarily archeological from excavations at English Camp, American Camp, and Belle Vue Sheep Farm, and related documentation. These collections are from field schools begun in 1946, which continued off and on until 1991. Both pre-contact and historic sites were excavated with pre-contact materials stored and managed at the Burke Museum (about 66,000 catalog numbers), and historic materials at North Cascades (38,000 catalog numbers) and Fort Vancouver (about 5,000 catalog numbers). The associated field documentation (recorded as archives) is located with the appropriate collections. The remainder of the collection is located at NOCA with the exception of a few bryophytes, insects, and paleontological specimens which are located at the Burke Museum, University of Washington.

Archeology	Ethnology	History	Archives	Biology	Paleontology	Geology	Total
402,072	0	3,847	519,838	2,693	310	81	928,841

Table 1 FY2009 Collections Management Report data

In 2005, a Museum Management Plan was completed for North Cascades National Park Service Complex and Ebey's Landing National Historical Reserve. Since the SAJH collections are managed by the NOCA curator and much of the collection is stored at the Marblemount Curation Facility, that plan addressed some of the issues that are relevant to the SAJH collection and are not repeated here. Issue C: Museum Facilities addresses concerns related to the Marblemount facility, and Issue F: Planning, Programming, and Staffing discusses the need to make the curator fulltime as well as for additional support costs to manage museum collections.

SAJH has three Operations Formulation System (OFS) requests in the system. All three specifically mention the need for additional support for the park's museum collection. Unfortunately, park priority 1 (25765A) is regional priority 68; the other two have not been prioritized by the region. When any of these requests, including priority 1, would be funded is unknown.

The park staff and the MMP team worked together over the course of the site visit to develop the issue statements contained in this plan. In addition, the team and key park staff met with Director Julie Stein and Assistant Archeology Collections Manager/NAGPRA Coordinator Megon Noble at the Burke Museum and with Chief of Cultural Resources Jesse Kennedy at NOCA about issues relating to the SAJH collections located at their respective institutions. Topics addressed meet the specific needs of San Juan Island National Historical Park as discussed during those meetings, and thus do not necessarily represent a complete range of collections management concerns.

Elements of this plan are developmental in nature. The recommendations are intended to guide the park through the process of refining and expanding the existing museum management program that supports all aspects of park operations, while at the same time providing guidelines for the growth and development of the museum management program. This plan is designed to assist the staff in continuing this process for the next five to seven years.

Members of the MMP team were selected for their ability to address specific needs and concerns of the park. Primary information gathering and the initial draft were developed over a two-week period in March 2009.

After the initial development of this plan, the concept of a multi-park facility to be located at FOVA was developed during discussions regarding the reuse of buildings being transferred to the National Park Service from the U.S. Army at Vancouver Barracks. The NPS has begun development of the East and South Vancouver Barracks Master Plan which will establish clear direction for the rehabilitation and public use of the East and South Barracks, which are due to be transferred in September 2011. In order to establish the NPS' needs for additional space for park museum collections, FOVA has completed an addendum to their 1998 Museum Management Plan (2010) that identifies a non-historic building (405) in South Barracks as the new facility for the park. Further, it concludes that, in conjunction with the regional strategy for consolidation of museum collections, this would be a good location for a network level facility to house museum collections. This plan has been revised to reflect that change in direction.

The team wishes to thank Superintendent Peter Dederich, former Chief of Resources Chris Davis, and Chief of Interpretation Mike Vouri for the courtesy, consideration, and cooperation extended during this planning effort. Their time, efforts, and involvement greatly facilitated the work, and are very much appreciated. These individuals obviously are dedicated and committed to the preservation of park resources, and it is a pleasure to work with such professionals.

Figure 1 Blockhouse and Commissary, English Camp, SAJH

Park Establishment

San Juan Island National Historical Park was established in 1966 to commemorate historical events that occurred on the island from 1853 to 1871 in connection with the final settlement of the Oregon Territory boundary dispute, including the so-called Pig War of 1859. This is the only site in the National Park System that illustrates, in its dramatic and largely intact physical setting, how war can be averted and peace maintained through positive action by individuals and governments.

Pressures had been building between the United States and Great Britain over possession of the San Juan Island group since 1846 when the Treaty of Oregon left ownership unclear. Precipitated by the shooting of a Hudson's Bay Company boar by American settler Lyman Cutlar in June of 1859, the conflict evolved into the "Pig War" crisis, at the height of which more than 500 U.S. Army soldiers and British Royal Marines supported by three British warships faced each other on San Juan Island's southern peninsula, within sight of the British colonial capitol of Victoria. After a tense standoff and some hurried diplomacy, officials on both sides restored calm and the nations agreed to a joint military occupation of the island until the boundary could be decided.

The American soldiers and British Royal Marines established their camps on opposite ends of the island, where they remained until Kaiser Wilhelm I of Germany, as arbitrator, awarded the islands to the United States in 1872. Today San Juan Island National Historical Park protects the historic camps and their cultural landscape settings and commemorates nearly 150 years of friendship between the United Sates, Great Britain, and Canada. The park also provides an excellent place to hike, picnic on the beach, experience wildlife, and enjoy a wealth of artifacts from these historic events.

Research and Excavation

The prehistory and early history of the island have been derived from the evidence obtained through archeological investigations. Additional information has been gathered through documents and research. The products of this research are the foundation of the San Juan Island NHP museum collections.

The first NPS archeological collections were generated by the University of Idaho (UI) archeological field school under annual cooperative agreements. UI excavations identified structures, features, and artifacts as part of the San Juan Island historic archeology survey, 1970-1978. Under the leadership of Dr. Roderick Sprague, UI excavated American Camp, Belle Vue Sheep Farm, San Juan Town, and English Camp. Steve Kenady analyzed pre-contact artifacts recovered from those excavations. Objects were cleaned, described, analyzed, and marked with field numbers for storage and exhibition at the UI Museum of Archeology in Moscow, Idaho.

Figure 2 Archeology at American Camp Parade Ground, 1970s

The research and excavation of historic sites led to the extensive pre-contact survey by the University of Washington (UW) archeological field school supervised by Dr. Julie Stein. Also, in multiple year contracts, UW conducted the pre-contact archeology survey at English Camp from 1983-1992. These excavations generated 27 accessions and 66,000 catalog records. Continuing research at the Burke Museum is reported from 1994 to 2009; formal reports have been written during this period. Artifacts from UW excavations are stored at the Burke Museum.

Bulk sediments from the British Camp excavations were temporarily stored in the UW Kane Hall basement from their collection in 1991-1992 until their move to NOCA in 2002. These need to be processed more thoroughly. The Burke Museum collections manager supervised data input from 1987 to 1994.

The passage of the Native American Graves Protection and Repatriation Act (NAGPRA) in 1991 has required the identification of human remains and associated funerary objects, a process which UW and NPS began with an inventory in 1993. The effort is close to resolution with repatriation to the Lummi Tribe completed in 2009. This effort has been accomplished by the Burke Museum NAGPRA coordinator and the NPS Pacific West regional anthropologist.

Collections Management

San Juan Island National Historical Park's local museum collection was managed by the SAJH Division of Interpretation since its establishment in 1966. Mostly used for interpretation, collected objects were retained at park headquarters, first at American Camp and later in a storage unit in Friday Harbor. A Division of Interpretation park ranger with collateral duties in museum reporting covered work with museum collections. In 1979, a trailer designed to be both the administrative building and visitor contact station was installed at American Camp. Park administrative headquarters moved to leased space in Friday Harbor in 1984, freeing the lobby for exhibit space. The San Juan Island NHP General Management Plan of 1978 called for cataloging and photographing the park museum collections. From 1980 through 1992, NPS curatorial funds were secured to continue cataloging archeological artifacts at UI and UW.

Documentation and Museum Management

A turning point for collection management at SAJH occurred in 1983. Through efforts of the Pacific Northwest regional curator and regional interpreter, work was started on a Scope of Collection Statement (SOCS). A SOCS was drafted and approved in 1983. It has been used as a working document ever since. In 1985, the park received assistance from the Pacific Northwest Regional Office (PNRO) in cleaning up the collection records. Items were cataloged; all Crook family items were removed from the park in 1987; and the park leased storage space in town for its museum collection. The Resource Management Division took over management of the collections in 1988.

The collaboration with University of Idaho came to a close in 1993. Collections excavated by UI and stored at UI were returned to NPS management and stewardship. Lacking its own storage facility, San Juan Island NHP entered into an agreement in 1993 with North Cascades National Park for storage of the San Juan Island historic archeology artifacts. Archeology objects and associated archival materials from the Belle Vue Sheep Farm, a Hudson's Bay Company farm on San Juan Island, are housed at the Northwest Cultural Resources Institute located at Fort Vancouver National Historic Site. The analysis of these objects will add depth to the story of fur trade farms, settlement patterns, and civilian - military interactions.

Staffing Improvements

Prior to 1994, North Cascades National Park (NOCA) hired seasonal employees to work with museum collections, usually as a collateral duty. A museum technician was hired in 1994 to manage the NOCA collections. At this time, responsibility for museum management moved into the NOCA Cultural Resource Branch of the Resource Management Division. The museum technician position was established as a permanent subject-to-furlough, upward-mobility journeyman position. An effort initiated in 1999 to professionalize and upgrade the museum technician to a museum curator position was accomplished in 2002.

In the early 1990s, responsibility for the SAJH collections was transferred to the management of the NOCA museum technician. Funds were allocated to supplement the salary of the part-time NOCA museum technician. In 1999, an agreement between NOCA and SAJH designated the NOCA curator as the curator-of-record for San Juan Island NHP. This action was partly in response to the regional requirement that a journeyman-level curator be assigned to administer park collections. The agreement has resulted in greatly improved management of the SAJH collections, and a corresponding decrease in the curatorial time available for the NOCA collections.

The NOCA museum program is presently in the Division of Resource Management. The Cultural Resource branch chief supervises the curator, while the curator is responsible for managing all aspects of the museum program. With budgets continuing to shrink, the museum program is considered to be in jeopardy. The curator position is subject-to-furlough, with NOCA paying 13 pay periods of 26 in a year. SAJH offers $13,000 a year for museum support. In 1995 SAJH payment equaled 13 pay periods of a lower-graded museum technician salary, but in 2009 this is less than four pay periods of a journeyman curator's salary. With increasing costs of inflation and career professionalization, the support SAJH offers the museum program is eroding.

New exhibits designed and built by park staff featuring historical archeology objects were installed in 1966 at the American Camp and Friday Harbor visitor contact sites. The San Juan Island NHP pre-contact archeology artifact collection and associated archives continues to be stored at the Burke Museum in Seattle. Research access to San Juan Island artifacts at the Burke Museum is the most extensive use of any of the San Juan Island collections.

A collection condition survey was completed by Tamsen Fuller in 1998. It was formulaic in approach, and followed a generic template which lacks the specificity to fully address the critical current issues. The half of the document entitled "Threats to Collections" is the same and as generic as every other collection condition survey contracted in the 1990s. Documentation and preservation treatments are recommended for about thirty museum objects. No conservation work has been accomplished. A collection condition survey was contracted in 2008 with the Burke Museum to document the San Juan Island NHP pre-contact lithic artifact collection in their care. The intent of the contract was three-fold: inventory the lithic artifacts, modify the database documenting the artifacts, and report on the storage, data, and artifact conditions. As of this writing, the contract is still in progress. The completion of the contract will see improved documentation; improved storage and the resultant data will assist research and improve inventory accountability.

Curator-of-Record

For several years, 1999-2003, the curator-of-record for SAJH invested the majority of time, dollars, and effort on the SAJH prehistory archeology collection. Agreements were entered into; University of Washington facility conditions were surveyed; artifact inventory was attempted at the Burke; and the Burke database for ANCS+ was corrupted and unusable.

During this time of fiscal belt-tightening, the recurrent theme of non-NPS institutions charging to house NPS museum collections arose nationwide. The SAJH pre-contact archeology collection at the Burke Museum Archeology Department at University of Washington was subject to the fee-storage review. However, the Burke never proposed that the SAJH collection be subject to such fees, given the use of the collection by staff, university employees, and students.

While touring the Burke collection, the curator documented non-secure and substandard facility conditions at the Burke Museum Archeology Department and Archeology Department storage located in Kane Hall. Environmental deficiencies and overcrowding of artifacts were observed in both building basements. Upon negotiation between the NPS and the Burke Museum, pre-contact artifacts for study remained at the Burke Museum; security and storage of NAGPRA–related artifacts were improved; and the Kane Hall sediment samples were moved to the SAJH collection at NOCA.

With the acceptance of bulk sediment samples from UW, more storage room was needed in Marblemount Curation Facility. Cabinets and cabinet tops were overcrowded and items spilled into the halls. With Museum Collection Protection and Preservation and Fee Demonstration funds, construction began on an adjoining 960 square foot collection storage room at the Curation Facility. Unfortunately, a lack of a storage plan compounded the overcrowding and the accountability deficiencies.

In 2002, the SAJH collections addition to the Marblemount Curation Facility was completed. The SAJH addition included cabinets mounted on mobile compacting storage carriages, making best use of the floor space available. The museum staff had begun the SAJH collections move from the North Cascades storage room. With the arrival of the current curator, the move was completed.

To assist in the move and get an idea of the extent of the historic archeology and bulk samples, the SAJH park superintendent and resource manager helped move SAJH artifacts from the NOCA storage room into the SAJH storage room. At the end of the move, the facility was full beyond safe capacity. An additional carriage, cabinets, and drawers have been purchased, installed, and filled as funding became available. A 100% inventory was conducted in 2005. Many artifacts transferred from UI to NOCA in 1995 were not located in the 2005 inventory. Those objects need a final, thorough investigation and a deaccession request may result.

In 2003, NOCA biologist Steve Hahn collected plants, pressed specimens, and documented the plant communities of San Juan Island NHP. The herbarium specimens offer baseline information for planning and mitigation in prairie restoration, Garry oak forest management, and landscape documentation. The herbarium data is shared with the North Coast and Cascades Inventory and Monitoring Network.

The Marblemount Curatorial Facility provides a research repository setting for researchers, educators, and park staff to come together to share knowledge and expertise, and to discuss current research in meetings, seminars, and classes.

Present and Future Collections Management Needs

The park has an approved Scope of Collection Statement. There is no staff for collections management work at SAJH. The park relies solely on the North Cascades National Park Service Complex's curator who, under signed agreement, serves as the curator-of-record for SAJH. Each year SAJH makes an attempt to provide funding to offset NOCA staff time, and since 2004, $13,000 was given annually to NOCA as reimbursement. SAJH has no storage capabilities for museum collections, so NOCA, FOVA, and the Burke Museum are serving as the repository for the artifacts. Additional collections management work will need to be done at SAJH, for many activities undertaken by the NPS will require compliance activities and rehabilitation work. These activities will likely result in more artifacts being added to the collection for documentation, review, and study. Funding for archives projects has been requested.

A general management plan/EIS was completed at SAJH in 2008. The needs of the staff relative to the collections are being addressed in the plan. The plan calls for the possibility of having a limited portion of the military-era artifacts, settlement-era artifacts, and natural resource specimens relocated to San Juan Island to an appropriately supervised and secure collections study room, in order to study these valuable assets in a local setting. The park is currently not planning to provide storage space and curatorial service. Collections will remain at the Burke Museum, FOVA, and NOCA until planning and any needed construction are complete for the multi-park facility at FOVA. At that time, materials will be moved from NOCA to FOVA. The extensive pre-contact archeological materials will remain at the Burke Museum. This is in line with the approved national curatorial facility strategy (2007).

Additional work in the collections includes UW prehistory excavation bulk sample analysis and sampling strategy. In the last year of the UW field school, an area was excavated with less processing at the site, with the assumption that culling would happen in the laboratory during analysis. It did not occur, and through inclusion of the collections without clear research plan or retention purpose, the bulk samples of sediment were added to the collections. A research design can make the collection ready for analysis and the bulk samples can be significantly reduced. With the disposal of some materials or reduction in the size of some samples, further research will improve collections data, collections quality, and collections management efficiency.

The mission of the research and collection management for the park is to foster the analysis, interpretation, and dissemination of information relating to history, archeology, archives, and historic architecture. The museum collection offers an unparalleled opportunity for study to researchers, students, and members of the public.

Issue Statement

Gaining intellectual control over the park's dispersed archival collections will facilitate access, communication, research, use, and exhibits.

Background

This issue explores the need to gain intellectual control over the park archives and information systems; the need to consolidate the management of the archives; and the steps required to make the information accessible to public and park researchers.

Archival records provide the framework for institutional memory. Park libraries contain published secondary-source materials, whereas archives contain primary source records related to park resources. Park records are documents, images, databases, maps, and informational resources that are created and used in park operations and administration. Park archives are derived from park records as well as non-park documents or images that meet the criteria for permanent retention as outlined in the current *DO#19: Records Management and Records Disposition Schedule*. Archives contain data regarding museum collections, park lands, historic structures, history, natural and cultural resources, and operations. These records are permanent because they embody the legacy of management and heritage that exists nowhere else. Proper control of records management is essential as a percentage of these active records will eventually become park archives. Accessibility and retrieval requires ongoing management from the moment records are created.

San Juan Island National Historical Park was established in 1966. SAJH has not had a previous collection or museum management plan. Based on the 2009 collection management report (CMR), the SAJH archives collection consists of 510,828 items with a backlog of about 9,000 items. The total research use for the 2009 fiscal year consisted of 54 requests from within the park and 20 from the public. When compared to other historical parks these statistics appear low and suggest that either not all of the requests are being documented, or more effort needs to be made to publicize the collections.

In 1985, the park's administrative history first makes mention of museum collections stored in a leased space in Friday Harbor. The vast bulk of associated records were created as part of the University of Idaho field work from 1970-1978, and the University of Washington field school from 1983-1991. Also, historical landscape study field work was conducted by Eastern Washington University. In 1992, the museum / archive collections at Idaho were transferred to NOCA at Marblemount. All Hudson's Bay Company (HBC) collections were sent to FOVA as part of the regional mission to consolidate the four separate Pacific Northwest HBC collections at one location.

The SAJH archives program is challenged by having collections stored at several different facilities and institutions. The curator-of-record for SAJH is located at North Cascades National Park (NOCA); no staff directly responsible for the collections is onsite at SAJH. For a park created in 1966, a much larger number of resource management records should be in the park archives. The 1997 SAJH Administrative History, written by Kelly June Cannon, stated "…in 1995, the author completed an assessment of park files for the creation of the park's administrative archive. This included a search of regional repositories, regional NPS files, and the National Archives and Records Administration. Unfortunately, the all-too-often heard story of files being thrown out to save space applies to SAJH NHP. Large gaps in the written record of park management have left some management decisions unexplained [undocumented]." Owing to proximity of the Pacific West Regional Office Seattle (PWRO-Seattle), there is some indication that SAJH resource management records may exist at that location. The park should investigate what records are there, and in particular, where the administrative archive collection was deposited.

The parks' administrative officer has kept all of the active park records in well-organized and labeled filing cabinets. As part of the MMP, the team archivist surveyed the records at the park. Six record boxes of SAJH archives are located at the National Archives and Records Administration (NARA) in Seattle. These have been microfilmed and copies provided to the park. SAJH has a microfilm reader and microfiche of the documents at NARA located in two boxes in the superintendent's office. All future resource management records are to be retained in the park archives and should not be sent to NARA.

Discussion

A survey of park records was conducted onsite as well as a review of archival materials located within the NOCA museum collection storage and the University of Washington's Burke Museum. The permanent materials still onsite at SAJH are still largely active or semi-active and have not been accessioned or cataloged. Archival collections at NOCA, FOVA, and the Burke have all been cataloged. Accession files at NOCA were also reviewed. The archives within the collection storage room are in good condition and appropriately housed. Since the bulk of the collections has been processed and cataloged, the focus will be on making the collections more accessible.

The park archives currently at SAJH and NOCA are comprised predominantly of resource management records, official records needed for ongoing management of resources at the park. This is typical of NPS archive collections. The park also has a large research and reference collection contained in the chief interpreter's office. The archives located at the Burke and at Fort Vancouver consists of associated records that document the artifacts and objects stored at these sites. They should continue to be kept in close proximity.

The Burke Museum has 35 LF of archives on loan from SAJH. These collections are field research and provenience data that document the artifacts and specimens from the park housed at the museum. The archival collections have been processed and cataloged into ANCS+ and a box and folder list finding aid has been created. Each collection is grouped by archeologist, and most span multiple field school years at the park. The associated records have only recently been cataloged and have not been easily accessible or researched by the NPS. The entire associated record collection at the Burke is essentially one collection (the field school) and each archeologist is a separate series. The only missing components for the collection are a "history" and "scope and content note" in the finding aid.

Once the multi-park facility at FOVA is active, SAJH will need to have a more formal archival survey that identifies and moves all inactive files to FOVA.

Once at FOVA, they need to be accessioned. The next step will be to process the collections to better preserve them, and then catalog the materials to make them accessible. As part of archival cataloging work, a finding aid will need to be created for each collection. Due to decentralized locations of the park's multiple collections, there are two critical issues. The first is that the curators of NOCA and FOVA will need good communication from all partners and SAJH in order to capture and organize all of the different archival components. The next will be to prioritize high use materials to be scanned and made accessible to all parties. Ideally, it would be good to have a centralized server or website which all other locations could access; otherwise, sending CDs of updated digital information would be necessary. It may be possible to FTP hardcopies, reports, and scans among the park and its partners; more technology will be discussed in Issue B.

Collections

The MMP team surveyed files at the American Camp visitor center and the Headquarters office. The Maintenance building was not surveyed and is the only other park site that could house files located in Friday Harbor. However, very few active files would have been at that location as the Maintenance building files were stored at the HQ. The San Juan Historical Museum, located at Friday Harbor, was not visited because the research center was undergoing rehabilitation at the time of the MMP site work. The historical museum is an informal partner with the park and has a number of photo and document collections pertaining to the history of the San Juan Islands. The SAJH chief interpreter is currently on the board for the museum. The SAJH accession log notates that museum objects were traded with the San Juan Historical Museum on at least one occasion. Formalizing the partnership and clarifying the role and function of the museum/archive programs at each site would help focus direction and avoid competition.

The American Camp visitor center has a few collections of primary source material that are archival. A filing cabinet of vertical and reference files is located in the chief interpreter's office. While the bulk of the documentation is secondary reference materials, primary source materials are interspersed. Much of the research involved in creating this collection required travel to other institutions, and the primary source materials tend to be the notes and writings of the chief interpreter, who has written several books related to the theme of the park. Even though these materials are largely secondary sources, because of the importance of the reference collection to the park, it would behoove the park to put the bulk of it into the custody of the museum and perhaps accession it. Under no circumstances should the primary sources be culled from the vertical files as that would undermine the integrity of the collection—the relationship of these materials is a key to its value. However, due to the value of the collection to the interpretation of the park, the transfer would need to be managed in a way that keeps these files accessible to SAJH staff. This would likely translate into needed materials being scanned prior to transfer to FOVA.

Figure 3 Historic photograph of American soldiers during occupation

Also located in the chief of interpretation's office is the park's historic photo collection. The collection of photographic prints and negatives has an organizational system that is not immediately intuitive. The coding system will need to be documented as best possible and included with the collection. The entire collection is archival and will need to be accessioned and transferred to FOVA for preservation and cataloging. Further investigation into origins and copyright of the photos will need to be done. Slides are located in the visitor center supply room on the top of cabinets to the right just upon entering through the door. They are housed in two archival boxes; staff mentioned they were likely archival. The park will need to determine if all of the images pertain to the site or if there are duplicates, as is often the case in interpretive slide files. If any of the slides are relevant to the park and have long term value, they should be added to the park archives, for they have already been scanned.

The active park central files are located at the park headquarters. Files span as far back as the 1970s, but for the most part, the bulk dates are 1990s to the present. In addition to central files, there are maintenance files regarding building documentation and site files, 106 compliance files, and some project files. A fair amount of resource management records (RMR) will need to be accessioned and archived, although the collection is still actively used. One option would be to pull RMR materials prior to 1995 and scan any of these files that the park feels are still actively used. The superintendent had a box of photographic prints on his desk. These were housed in NPS manila envelopes and were primarily photo documentation of sites and work within the park (maintenance related). These are RMR and should be accessioned and archived in the near future.

A flat file cabinet with maps, plans, and aerial photos is located in the headquarters office. These items are largely inactive, and drawings which have not yet been sent to the Technical Information Center (TIC) in Denver. They need to be sent to insure that they are microfilmed and digitized. When sending the plans to TIC, the park should include a receipt for property and instruct TIC to return the hardcopies to the park once completed. SAJH will need to add all of the returned plans to the museum collection archives upon return. A few SAJH drawings are listed on the e-TIC database, although more items may be at TIC and just not immediately accessible. They have either not yet been scanned, or are indexed with names other than SAJH (for example the search may require using a wide variety of terms such as Pig War, Friday Harbor, English Camp, American Camp, and so on).

TIC also has the capability to scan the NARA microfiche which would make it more accessible to a wider audience. The park should contact TIC to determine if an index exists of all SAJH documents at TIC and for rates and deals that could be arranged to digitize the maps and microfiche at the park.

The SAJH archival materials located at the NOCA and Burke Museum are in very good condition. Only a few preservation concerns need to be addressed. Rolled plans, photos, and drawings will need to be relaxed by a conservator. Any files or documents within archival document boxes that are falling over or slouching will need to have buffered spacers placed into the boxes to prevent this curvature. A few of the boxes are overfilled with documents. The catalog records for the SAJH archival collections have one nuance that should be rectified and avoided in the future. A review of the catalog record blue cards revealed that the "object field" had been consistently used with a classification term instead of the actual title. For example, many of the catalog records were listed as "Newspaper" when it would be better to list the title "Seattle Times, 1987, Re-enactment at SAJH."

The museum needs to attract more research use. This can be accomplished by creating exhibits, providing more documentation and visibility via the website, and strengthening partnerships. An example would be to have the Burke host an exhibit on SAJH archeology. The next step to increase research use is to actively pursue museum and archive donations, such as letters, photos, drawings, journals, and accoutrements from private donors. The final step is for SAJH staff to research their own collections and publicize the holdings. Time should also be spent researching the provenience and history of objects and previously acquired archival documentation. In addition, it would be useful for the park to research the relevant holdings of other institutions.

The 1997 SAJH Administrative History lists some repositories that contained relevant collections: Washington State Archives in Olympia, Washington State Historical Society library, UW manuscript library, and Eastern Washington University (Historic Landscape Study field work). The MMP team archivist established leads for other documentation, including the Canadian Provincial Archives at Victoria, the Hudson's Bay Company Archives in Winnipeg, and Historian Gretchen Luxenberg's Historic Resource Study files, likely still at the PWRO-Seattle office.

The curator-of-record (COR) has been tasked with a large work load for three distinct parks, with emphasis on managing the archives, museum collections, and libraries, and providing assistance to researchers. In addition, other responsibilities include exhibits, outreach, record-keeping, preservation, and cataloging, to name a few. The position is currently funded at .5 FTE and relies heavily on soft funding, even though the workload warrants at least 1 FTE at the full professional level (GS-11). The curator position will continue to be challenged to manage successfully the entire NOCA and EBLA museum program without a stronger commitment to full time. A more effective staffing solution would be to increase the base-funded position to 1 FTE and then use the soft funded projects for seasonal museum staff.

Records Management

In the last two decades, records management has become a crucial issue at most parks. While the administrative officer is ultimately responsible for official records at the park, parks have no official records managers, and these duties are largely collateral. For the central files system to be effective, the creator of records must enter the correct central file code.

Incorrect coding can lead to erroneous dispositions of potentially critical records. *Director's Order #19* has been superseded in the last year by a newer version that identifies the resource management records which are to be archived at the park. This current version is available at the Inside NPS website.

While the central file system is still an effective tool for managing administrative records, recently NPS archivists and records managers have advised park divisions to begin implementing a project checklist approach to managing records. Instead of assigning central file codes to documents, the project checklist relies on the creators of project files to keep the project intact and label the files in such a way that they are clearly tied to an over-arching project. Managing records as projects is much more effective, and once inactive, these collections are easier to appraise and make accessible as they are accessioned into the park archives. This will become even more critical regarding electronic records management. See Appendix D for project checklist templates. The project management approach would be ideal for upcoming SAJH projects such as the Prairie Restoration, Forest Restoration, and Butterfly Study projects.

The park will need to develop a policy for managing and migrating analog items, digital files, and databases with accompanying metadata. Metadata is data that is used to describe the image, raster file, or database and must be preserved. In regards to digital images, metadata is the "who, what, when, where, and how" documentation, such as the photographer, subject, date, and so on. Metadata is often lost or unusable when printed to hardcopy, so the park needs to contemplate the management and organization of digital and electronic filing prior to creation (or soon thereafter).

The park will be truly effective in this only if it requires all park staff to receive necessary training, and receives a commitment from park management to enforce already applicable records management policies and procedures. If these are not adhered to, the costs to retrieve obsolescent technology becomes astronomical and critical baseline data and institutional history will disappear.

The long-term objective for the park should focus less on having a designated records manager for the entire park, and more on having individual staff members responsible for their own records. To help achieve this goal, the park should have a records management training for all employees. One of the premiere records managers within the NPS is based at Golden Gate National Recreational Area (GOGA). It is advisable to have Susan Ewing Haley from GOGA lead the records management training, and consult with the park on records management issues.

In the interim, the park should avoid the disposition or shredding of any park files without the assistance of an NPS field archivist. Due to the lack of records managers within the NPS, appraisal and scheduling disposition has largely become the responsibility of archivists who can easily ascertain temporary files from permanent, explain retention periods, and determine where materials should be sent (i.e., NARA, the park archives, or the recycle bin). The park needs to document decisions that are not readily available in writing and place these in the accession files.

SOPs and Protocols

The main obstacle for the park's museum program is communication and accessibility. All of the locations that hold SAJH museum and archive collections are some distance from the park, which is an issue for research use and park staff. Intellectual control over these components requires them all to be identified and organized using a finding aid and database. With the advent of technology, the collections do not need to be in close physical proximity to each other in order to be accessible. As part of this organization, agreements between the park and all partners need to be up-to-date and clarify roles and responsibilities. Methods for improving communication and technology will be described in Issue B of this plan.

The job of organizing all of this information is not solely the responsibility of the curator-of-record. A more realistic approach would be for the curator-of-record to be the gatekeeper for the information and responsible for helping disseminate updates and requests to the respective partners and SAJH staff. To facilitate this, all MOUs, MOAs, SOPs, contracts, and agreements will need to be compiled into one distinct group with the originals archived and scans or copies produced for onsite SAJH use. The curator-of- record will need to be kept apprised of projects and changes at SAJH and will need access to PMIS, PEPC, research permits, and I&M data. The curator-of-record would be responsible for providing the park with updated CDs, access to databases such as ANCS+, and other pertinent information. Instead of relying on email and/or mail, it would be wise to have face-to-face meetings on a bi-annual basis and have a receipt of property (or some other formalized procedure) to track the progress and level of communications.

Library

The SAJH library is small and is managed by the park's interpretive staff. A few rare books are housed in the chief interpreter's office. Depending on the value and rarity of the books, it would be worth exploring if they should be accessioned into the museum Automated National Catalog Systems (ANCS+) and then loaned back to the user. The library also includes a very small audio/visual collection. As part of improving accessibility and communication, it would be good to have a volunteer keep the library up-to-date in the NPS Voyagers system (previously Procite), or some other system that park staff and partners could access. No funding is currently available for the park to acquire new books or periodicals. Increases to the holdings are added by contributions, typically from Northwest Interpretive Association.

Recommendations

- Identify, accession, and move into the SAJH park archives all permanent records at the visitor center and park headquarters for preservation and protection at FOVA.

- Digitize files and images so that they are accessible to SAJH staff.

- Research and identify other pertinent SAJH potential archives at the PWRO-Seattle, the Technical Information Center, and any other possible locations.

- Implement a formal records and electronic records management program.

- Provide records management training for all staff.

- Identify institutions and universities where relevant collections are located.

- Develop and implement protocols and standard operating procedures for managing and communicating among all holdings of the SAJH collections.

- Research SAJH holdings to better understand provenience of the collections and the content of the holdings.

  1. Conduct proactive outreach to acquire new donations, raise awareness of the park's holdings, and increase park research use.

  2. Ensure the curator-of-record's access to PMIS, PEPC, and the research permits issued by SAJH as part of better communications and participation.

- Investigate a more formal partnership with the San Juan Historical Museum and work to avoid any overlap in mission or scope of collections.

- Revise draft Scope of Collection Statement with regard to archives.

- Compile all park MOUs, MOAs, SOPs, and contracts and agreements into one distinct grouping.

- Create a finding aid with a "scope and content note" and a "history" section for the associated records at the Burke.

- Conduct an oral history with current Burke Museum director Julie Stein.

Figure 4   Exhibit case, American Camp Visitor Center, SAJH

Issue B—
Exhibit and Use

Issue Statement

The park can maximize access and use of collections by emphasizing artifact-based learning techniques and incorporating technological innovations.

Background

The dispersed location of the collections has been summarized previously in this document. One result of this dispersal is the lack of ready access to collections for both staff and visitors. The park currently functions with an outdated interpretive plan (1984) which does not reflect the interpretive themes presented in the park's 2008 General Management Plan. This section discusses some of the possibilities for increasing access and use of the collection through available technologies and careful design based on the themes suggested in the GMP.

Exhibits - The main opportunity for public access to the park's collections is the English Camp visitor center. Open year-round, this "temporary" facility consists of a double-wide trailer installed in 1979. The visitor center contains three cases of artifacts: two house historical archeology artifacts from the American and English Camps and the third case contains artifacts from pre-contact Native American settlements. The cases are older and do not have environmental controls to protect the artifacts. There is no clear delineation between the interpretive exhibits and the park's bookstore/gift shop area..

Other exhibit features include a replica American uniform and a video laserdisc slideshow. A poster about the natural resources of the park is located in the corner. According to park staff, archeological staff at the Burke Museum developed an interpretive poster for the park, but it is not on display because it is perceived by park staff as too visually dense. A contact station, open only during the summer, is located in the historic English Camp barracks; it also contains a slideshow and a visitor information counter. The GMP calls for rehabilitation of part of the barracks for combined use, including an interpretive exhibit.

Interpretation - The park's interpretive program schedules a lively summer calendar. Events include an annual historic reenactment, a number of pioneer skills demonstrations, naturalist walks, theatrical and musical performances, and an annual archeology walk. Some programs are offered for school groups. The most developed offering concerns the Pig War, and is supported by a traveling trunk that teachers may use to prepare their classes beforehand. The trunk also includes a thorough resource guide with curriculum topics broken down according to Washington State Essential Academic Learning Requirement guidelines. In addition to the park's mandated themes of conflict resolution through arbitration, the park's interpretive programming also includes some artifact-based learning using historical archeology objects. There are two short archeology programs: a 30-minute version at English Camp focuses on the site's pre-contact cultures, and a 15-minute talk about protecting archeology resources utilizes the display case in the American Camp visitor center.

Research access - No statistics are being collected by the park about the frequency of research requests for the park's artifacts or archives collections at the park. Research requests are usually directed to Chief of Interpretation Mike Vouri, both because of his status as an historical expert on the Pig War and his office's location at the American Camp visitor center. As noted previously, the curator is also frequently on furlough, making consistency in response to research requests an issue. No information is listed on the park's website as to where research requests should be directed, or the type and extent of the park's collections. The Burke Museum does collect statistics on collection use as part of its MOU obligation with the park; the 2008 annual report to the park recorded 12 instances of access by 28 people for research and tours.

The 2008 GMP refers to an online ANCS+ catalog with 1,000 digital images as available to the public. Though the GMP refers to this online aspect of the catalog as functional, this is not the case. The park's ANCS+ (now ICMS) database is housed at the NOCA Marblemount facility for use by the curator, who sends regular backup discs of the collection to the park's office in Friday Harbor. Online access at the park's visitor facilities has been upgraded to broadband Internet. No public access to the ICMS database is currently available at the visitor facilities or online, but the capability now exists.

There is a current PMIS request for funds to catalog the photographic collection. A digital photography project slated to occur this summer will add an extra 300 artifact images to the current 1,000 images which are contained in the ANCS+ database. A large number of the catalog entries pertaining to archeological artifacts are minimally labeled, which casts doubt on the usefulness of making this information available. However, a cooperative inventory monitoring project for the archeological collection at the Burke Museum also includes re-cataloging these collections to include more specific information about each artifact.

Issue D of this document discusses a proposal currently under consideration by the park that would transfer the park's collections currently kept at the North Cascades Marblemount facility to a proposed new facility at Fort Vancouver (FOVA). The FOVA facility would house collections from multiple parks.

Discussion

The 2008 GMP reflects a number of interpretive themes that differ from the previous 1984 interpretive plan. Most notable is the addition of archeological and natural resource themes to the park's primary theme of interpreting the boundary dispute and conflict resolution. Though only two GMP interpretive themes mention the park's collections specifically, the archeological, natural history, and historical collections offer ample opportunities to support interpretation with tangible evidence.

The GMP also calls for internet access to collections, innovative methods of "virtual" experiences, and a web catalog. A new interpretive plan is needed to fully incorporate the interpretive themes expressed in the GMP, including exhibit strategies for the anticipated American Camp visitor center and a plan for regular review of exhibit content and conditions. Ideally, this plan would utilize digital and social media technologies while reinforcing the power of direct experience with both the landscape and its associated artifacts. It should also incorporate design elements that will work together to provide an integrated experience for park visitors as well as provide accessibility for a wide range of audiences.

Digital technologies will be helpful in meeting the challenges of access presented by the remote location of the park and the dispersion of its collections. However, these should not replace the primary function of museum collections, which is to support learning based on interaction with artifacts. Online techniques function best when they are supplementing visits to a park rather than replacing them. Smart and creative project design helps to ensure that the park uses methods that are both suited to its particular needs and capable of fulfilling multiple functions.

With the near-constant introduction of new technologies, there is a tendency in the museum world to pursue the newest and shiniest rather than pursuing appropriately strategic technologies to meet institutional needs. The park should be cautious in how these projects are approached and think creatively about how tools might function together. The sustainability of any digital project is also an important consideration. Will interpretive staff or curation staff be required to maintain these programs? Have staff members been appropriately trained on all the technological aspects that may be required? Will the appropriate infrastructure be provided? However, online technologies do present some relatively simple ways to increase access to the collections and the research generated by studying them.

The online database, which the park is already planning on installing, is a good example of this latter category. For the database to be usable inside the park, computer workstations and high speed internet cable for the visitor center and contact station will need to be installed. If the park is serious about encouraging on-site research, ready access to the database will be particularly important. Support for the ICMS database is recommended as a basic step for guaranteeing public access to the collections.

The Harper's Ferry Center High Resolution Digital Imaging Project performed work in the Marblemount facility during FY2009. This project will produce another 300 images for inclusion in the database. These images will provide an excellent resource for online interpretative projects. Once the Burke Museum inventory project is completed, more useful information will be available about the objects from English Camp archeological excavation "Op A." However, the estimated 1,300 images that eventually will be available represent only a small portion of the collection. Much of the archeological collection at the Burke Museum is debitage and flake, which are not particularly photogenic. The park will need to implement some criteria about which artifacts are worthy of the time spent on photography, and to schedule regular updates of the database, which will require curatorial support. The database will also need to be easily found on the park's webpage in order to ensure public use.

Fort Vancouver NHS provides an excellent model for encouraging public access to research and collections. A "quicklink" on the park's webpage leads to a separate collections and research homepage. This would be a good place to link to the online database, as well as to any reports or research that are generated through the park's collections. A bibliography of published books by researchers who have used the collection (such as Mike Vouri and Julie Stein) should also be included, as well as links to the Burke Museum's online collections. Though the Burke Museum's archeology collection is not currently online, the museum herbarium has an excellent online database that refers to specimens from the park. This online research area should also include the research request form, which could be then be digitally submitted and used to generate access statistics. It should also plainly detail the type of collections held by the park and some general information about the collections held by each repository.

Another opportunity for multifunctional design is presented by the need for new exhibits in the visitor center. These exhibits have been accumulated piecemeal over time and do not present an integrated narrative about the meaning of the displayed artifacts in relation to the park's history. The cases, which need to be replaced, contain only minimal information about the artifacts. The information is not immediately apparent due to its location on the side of the cases. The poster displays appear worn, and the laserdisc slideshow is outdated.

Concern that new exhibits or other investment in the current visitor center will interfere with proposals for a new visitor center is valid. But allowing the current exhibits to remain outdated fails to serve the educational needs of current park visitors and reflects poorly on the NPS. Designing new exhibits intelligently with an eye to how they could be easily integrated into the new visitor center would be a better solution. The same premise could be applied to exhibit cases for the English Camp contact station. Small moveable cases with environmental controls could be displayed during the summer months, and removed during the off season to provide adequate security. These cases could be integrated into a traveling exhibit about the park available to area historical societies and libraries.

A subtle but significant concern is the appearance of intermixing of merchandise with artifacts in the visitor center. This habit reduces the importance of the collection's artifacts. By the very nature of being held in perpetual trust for the public, NPS collections require being held apart as very special kinds of materials. The encroachment of the book store into the exhibits detracts from the impact of the collection's very reason for being. Placing artifacts on the contact station's mantel reinforces the public's perception of archeological artifacts as trophies to be collected.

Though these artifacts are not suitable for accession into the research collection, they could be consolidated into an education collection which could be used for artifact-based learning. This education collection could also meet the GMP's call for a "study collection" at the park. Education collections generally contain objects that are not appropriate for research collections because of poor provenience or general abundance and thus do need not be handled as strictly as research collections. The establishment of an education collection would be very helpful in incorporating more artifact-based learning into the interpretive program.

One learning method the park is already using that could be easily expanded is the learning trunk program. The Burke Museum archeology staff has already produced two such trunks for Seattle's Discovery Park, and has expressed enthusiasm over the prospect of collaborating on an archeology trunk for San Juan NHP. One of the Discovery Park trunks stays on site and is used for park ranger programs there. Similar instructional kits could be developed for different interpretive themes in the park, including archeology, historical archeology, ecosystem, and paleontology. The education collection could easily be incorporated into these kits. A unique paleontological collection of Pleistocene marine fossils from the park is housed at the Burke Museum; casts could be made of these fossils to be included in the trunk. One of the most important parts of the trunks meant for classroom use is the inclusion of Essential Academic Learning Requirements (EALR) curriculum prompts. These have become critical for museum outreach in Washington State, as teachers now must fulfill specific criteria in their curriculum. Including EALR guidelines makes it easy for teachers to use the trunks, creating a much better chance that classes will actually have an opportunity to make a field trip to the park.

The interpretive themes included in the GMP offer a range of possibilities for exhibits in the anticipated new visitor center. Taken together, these themes call for a holistic presentation of the natural history of the island and humans' place in that history. The park's current interpretive program focuses mainly on the primary theme set out by the establishing legislation, which is the boundary dispute and its settlement by diplomacy and arbitration. The GMP expands desirable interpretive themes to include natural resources, cultural landscapes, post-military settlement, and archeological resources. The new visitor center will provide an opportunity to expand the interpretation to include these themes. It will also provide an opportunity to interpret ongoing projects in the park and their importance.

Discussion of the island's natural resources should include human impacts, current prairie and Garry oak forest ecology restoration efforts, and the return of the Island Marble butterfly. These exhibits will provide a good opportunity to discuss why prairie restoration efforts became necessary, the impact of invasive species, and the adaptation of the Island Marble butterfly to new habitats. Information about the island's rich natural resources will support presentations about the presence of pre-contact residents and their settlement patterns.

The GMP also encourages partnerships with tribal members for preparation of exhibits and programming about Native American connections to the island. Interpretation of the boundary dispute should include discussion of the impact of Euro-American settlement on Native American inhabitants and continue the history-to-present-day situations. Exhibits interpreting the boundary dispute also present opportunities for contextualization of the dispute within larger themes, not only of the current focus on arbitration and diplomacy, but also settlement and exploration of the Pacific Coast, the effect of European contact on native peoples, and subsequent ecological impacts.

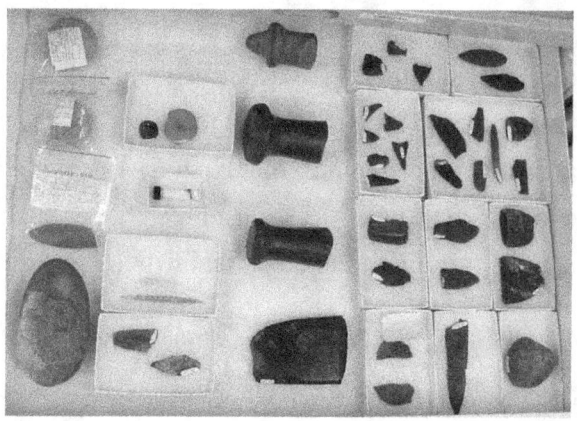

Figure 5 Lithics in storage at the Burke Museum

The park will also need to plan for regular updates of exhibits. Smaller project-oriented exhibits dependent on current information will need to be reviewed and updated every one to three years (for example, the suggested exhibits about prairie restoration and the Island Marble butterfly). Larger exhibits that focus on major interpretive themes such as the boundary dispute and pre-contact habitation should be reviewed and updated every seven to ten years to reflect new research and additions to the collection. Any technological elements in the exhibits will need to be reviewed on a tighter ongoing basis to ensure their functionality and relevance.

However, the park's limited staffing resources could obstruct the exhibit maintenance cycle. Building the partnerships emphasized in other sections of this document could also present opportunities to gather assistance for keeping exhibits current, particularly in regard to keeping on top of technological elements. One option might be to recruit museum studies interns from the University of Washington or other museum studies programs, though a stipend would need to be provided to assist with travel and housing. The Burke Museum and the Washington State History Museum both have active exhibit departments that may be interested in building partnerships with the park.

If the park decides to move its collections to the proposed joint curation facility at FOVA, there will be significant opportunities to collaborate with other parks that have collections relating to the history of the Hudson Bay Company in the Pacific Northwest. FOVA is known for its energetic outreach to its urban community, and there may be exciting opportunities to create jointly managed programs. However, the challenge of remaining connected to the park's collections may also increase along with the physical distance between on-site staff and the museum collections. To maximize the benefit of such a decision, SAJH staff will need to engage proactively on collaborative planning for outreach, interpretive, and curation activities. Regular travel should be budgeted for curation and interpretive staff to facilitate one-on-one interaction as part of management and interpretation of the collection. With these steps, commitment to a joint curation facility will be part of growing the park's presence rather than passing off its curation responsibilities.

Recommendations

- Program for a new interpretive plan which should include emphasis on artifact-based learning and incorporation of appropriate new technologies.

- Complete necessary steps to launch the online ICMS database, including a policy prioritizing objects for photography, a regular schedule for refreshing the database, and funding the appropriate curatorial support.

- Install ICMS workstations at both visitor centers, supported by high-speed internet access.

- Create a separate area in the park's webpage for collections and research that can be used to launch the online database, publish reports, provide a research bibliography, and track research requests.

- Collaborate with the Burke Museum to produce traveling trunks with archeological, ecological, and paleontological themes.

- Program for new exhibits for the visitor center which can be translated easily into the future new facility.

- Collaborate with the Burke Museum to produce a dual-purpose traveling exhibit that can also be used in the English Camp contact station during summer months.

- Consolidate any artifacts lacking provenience into an educational collection to be used for hands-on learning.

- Research new technologies thoroughly to determine their suitability and sustainability within the park.

Figure 6 Bryophyte storage, Burke Museum

San Juan Island National Historical Park Museum Management Plan

Issue Statement

Improving documentation of San Juan Island National Historical Park collections will help the park attract new research relevant to both management and cultural resource disciplines.

Background

The SAJH collection is comprised of archives (discussed in Issue A), arachnology, botanical specimens, paleontology specimens, historical objects and archeology items. The arachnology, botany, paleontology, and history collections are relatively small while the archeology assemblages total roughly 98.5% of the total collection. The collections from National Park Service managed property on San Juan Island were generated primarily through directed inventory and research projects. A few artifacts and specimens were brought into the Visitor Center and contact station by visitors. However, these items have not been incorporated into the general SAJH collections. Thus, the SAJH collections are complete with records describing collecting methods, object history, and adequate spatial information. Due to the general adherence to ethics concerning collecting and the park's identified collection scope, the various assemblages generated from work at SAJH are ideal for future research and current interpretive programs.

This chapter describes the composition of the SAJH collection and discusses the need for basic documentation of archeological materials in order to generate a greater breadth of research interest.

Description of San Juan Island National Historical Park Collections

Arachnology: The few specimens include spiders, butterflies, and moths. The spiders were collected by Rod Crawford at the Burke Museum of Natural History and Culture but there is no park permit or other information associated with this assemblage. The rest of the arachnology collection (totaling 20 specimens) was generated by Robert Michael Pyle's research on butterflies. His field work did include a park research and collecting permit and was used to write *The Butterflies of Cascadia: A Field Guide to all the Species of Washington, Oregon and Surrounding Territories* (2002), Seattle Audubon Society.

Botany: These assemblages include vascular plants and bryophytes. There are no planned forays intended to increase representative botany specimens even though other groupings (lichens, fungi, and algae) are not included as voucher specimens in the SAJH botany collection. According to David Giblin, Ph.D. (Burke Museum Herbarium Collection Manager) the SAJH botany specimens housed at the Burke Museum of Natural History and Culture are used as a research collection for both on-site analysis as well as loaned items for study. The SAJH items also act as voucher specimens for the distribution of the different taxa and were the basis for a publication of *Moss Flora of the Pacific Northwest* (1971) by Elva Lawton.

Collection	Facility	Assemblage Description	No. of Cataloged Items
Botany	Marblemount Curation Facility	Vascular Plants	597
	The Burke Museum of Natural History and Culture	Bryophytes	268
		Vascular Plants (Sharon Rodman)	21
Arachnology	The Burke Museum of Natural History and Culture	Spiders (Rod Crawford), Butterflies and Moths (Robert Michael Pyle)	20
Paleontology	The Burke Museum of Natural History and Culture	Invertebrates (David Delthier Pleistocene Era specimens (totaling 308)	38
Archeology	Marblemount Curation Facility	Op D from English Camp, Sprague's Historical Archeology, UW field notes (copies), UI field notes (original)	28,497
	FOVA	Belle Vue Sheep Farm and Associated Records from Sprague (UI) excavation	5,260
	The Burke Museum of Natural History and Culture	Pre-contact Archeology from Cattle Point, English Camp	70,490
	American Camp VC Exhibit	Pre-contact and Historic Archeology	182
History	Marblemount Curation Facility	Crook Family History (objects only)	216
		Architectural Fragments and Plans	55
		Crook House Family English Camp Negatives	36

Table 2   Location of SAJH collections, 2009

Paleontology: This collection is comprised of Pleistocene Era invertebrates that were collected by David Delthier in 1996. This assemblage is housed at the Burke Museum of Natural History and Culture and is periodically used by students, instructors, and researchers because it is one of the few invertebrate collections and one of the only assemblages of marine fossils from the Pleistocene Era.

History: This collection is comparably ad hoc with some items picked up by former park employees. The woodworking tools and other objects from the Crook family represent a cohesive assemblage of items from the settlement period. Most of these objects are in good condition and would be useful for the interpretation of the settlement period. Other history objects include architectural fragments and plans collected by historical architects working to restore buildings at English Camp (LaFleur 1977) and American Camp (Carper 1977).

Archeology: These assemblages span several thousand years of the Island's human occupation. Much of the archeology collection, though, is from the historical period associated with the nationally significant context and events for the establishment of the park. The historical archeology is associated with the Pig War, the Hudson's Bay Company occupation near American Camp, and San Juan Town. These assemblages were generated through a University of Idaho historical archeology field school conducted each summer from 1970 to 1977. Analysis of the recovered artifacts took several more years.

The final archeology report for excavations at English Camp (45-SJ-24), San Juan Town (45-SJ-290), Hudson's Bay Company Belle Vue Farm (45-SJ-295) and American Camp (45-SJ-300) was completed in 1983 (Sprague et al. 1983). This work has contributed an enormous amount of information for the interpretation of regional history and should not be overlooked as potential information for broader anthropological questions. Based on a recent cursory inspection for the North Cascades and Ebey's Landing Museum Management Plan (2005), the artifacts and associated records for the Pig War and Hudson's Bay Company sites have been fully processed and are in stable housing. According to the historical archeologist at Fort Vancouver (Cromwell personal communication 2009) a few artifact classes have not been fully analyzed and are under-reported. Other artifact classes are generally lacking in detail compared to current standards.

Sixteen pre-contact archeology sites are identified and partially documented within the SAJH boundary. Of these sites, two have been investigated through sub-surface excavation. The Cattle Point Site (45-SJ-1) was excavated in 1950 by Arden King. The historical component at English Camp was excavated as an Idaho State University field school (Sprague 1973) and the shell middens at and adjacent to English Camp were excavated as a University of Washington archeology field school from 1984 to 1991. The pre-contact component field school was directed by Julie K. Stein, Ph.D., at the University of Washington.

The excavations generated a large volume of shell and sediment samples because the loci investigated by the University of Washington were shell middens. This approach to shell midden excavation was unique for the region and the collection now stands as one of the few sites that retained excavated bio-samples. While many collection managers are weary of managing the upkeep of these types of collections, the recent analysis of eco-facts to address contemporary issues (e.g. local shifts in climate and nutritional equivalencies) has proven to be extremely valuable. During the final field season in 1991 the field processing methods changed. The strategy for excavation that season was to excavate units at Operation D and finish processing the materials at the University. In sum, many of the excavated materials have yet to be processed and analyzed.

Recent Research and the Potential for Future Studies

The potential use of collections for exhibit, marketing, and research has been discussed in a number of publications (e.g. Childs 2007, McKenzie et al. 1997, Kotler 1999). Many National Park Service museum programs in the Pacific West Region have not kept pace with private or university affiliated museums in updating exhibits, creating new outreach materials or conducting research on assemblages. This is in part due to previous inventory or documentation approaches that directed all funds toward data and specimen collecting instead of balancing the collecting with curating for the generated assemblage. Projects that did not provide support for collection care have left unprocessed and poorly described materials for NPS curators to manage. At SAJH the incomplete state of material processing and artifact description of the archeology collection may be hampering their use for current research.

While a considerable amount of archeological material has not been processed or analyzed from the pre-contact sites at English Camp, reporting on-site findings has provided important insights into the culture history of the Pacific West coast. Other than annual letter reports from Stein to the NPS about progress made each field season, three published books that describe and interpret the archaeological material from excavations at SAJH are currently available to researchers and the public: *Deciphering a Shell Midden* (Stein 1992), *Exploring Coast Salish Prehistory: The Archaeology of San Juan Island* (Stein 2000) and *Finding the People who Flaked the Stone at English Camp (San Juan Island)* (Close 2006). A book concentrating on the interpretation of a horseshoe shaped shell midden at English Camp (Op D) is currently being edited by Julie Stein. A few academic articles that discuss archeological accumulation rates (Stein et al. 2002) and the effects of the "marine reservoir" on dating shell (Deo et al. 2004) also use materials excavated from English Camp. A recent doctoral dissertation (Daniels, 2009) used materials excavated from Op D at English Camp to construct a new model for foraging behavior and gender to identify a higher quality marine environment for resources commonly exploited by women (like shellfish).

More descriptive information about the composition of the SAJH archeology collections combined with active outreach to attract different types of research could greatly improve our understanding of human adaptations to changing environments and human impacts to their surroundings. Many current research topics in archeology are attempting to provide more information about past human experiences instead of simply documenting culture history in the region. Research on environmental shifts, disease, nutrition, and landscape change are currently being pursued by archaeologists because of the expectation of changes that will impact contemporary people. Shell midden sites in the Pacific Northwest lend themselves to this research. This is in part due to good preservation of perishable materials in middens because of the alkaline environment created by the concentration of shell. The high concentration of materials from human activity also acts as proxy data for nutritional analysis and impacts by humans on the landscape.

Research on the presence and management of parasites by people living in the past has been conducted using midden remains (Bathurst, 2005). Descriptions of nutritional quality (Anderson, unpublished data) have also been attempted using midden shells collected during previous excavation. Assessing impacts from climate change is also re-emerging as a significant topic applicable to current island residents.

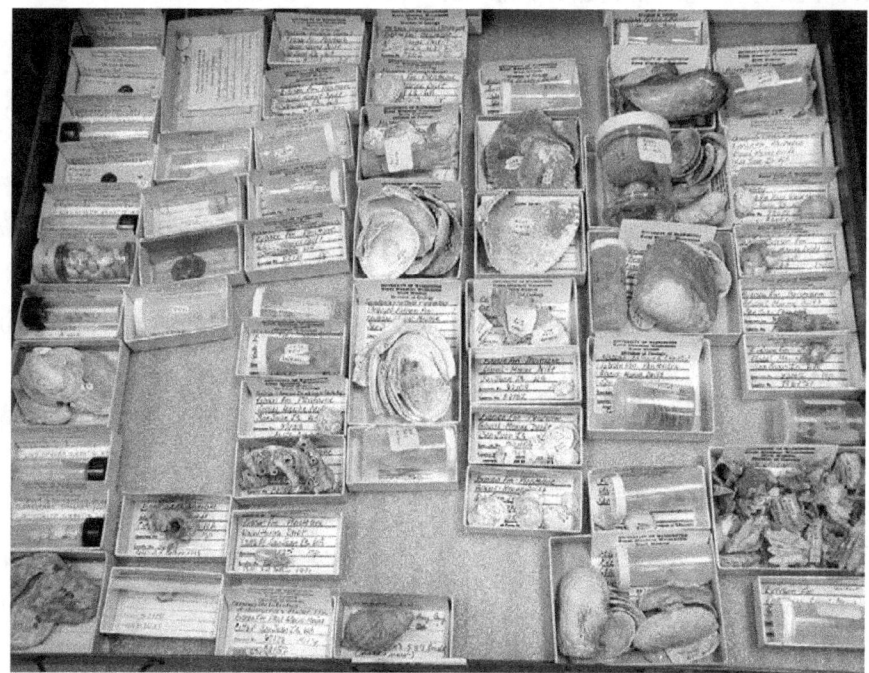

Figure 7   Pleistocene shells from SAJH at the Burke Museum

Advances in analytical instruments also play a role in the types of studies that can be pursued using collections. The rapid improvement to techniques used for identifying isotopic signatures has resulted in a wide range of potential research not considered when the collections were originally generated. Radiocarbon dating (one type of isotope analysis) has been refined and other forms of isotope analysis (e.g. oxygen used to identify a place of origin; carbon and nitrogen used in assessing past staples in the human diet; strontium and lead helping to determine migrations) continue to improve. The technology used to approach questions concerning diet, migration, and source will continue to improve.

Other advances in material analysis include x-ray fluorescence (XRF). This technique is frequently referred to as 'chemical fingerprinting' because it identifies the source area of materials found in objects of antiquity. The application of XRF to stone is a reliable way to identify the source of the lithic material and could also be helpful in the analysis of many of the glass and metal historical archeology objects. The source area of much of the stone used in the production of tools on the Northwest coast is poorly understood, so this type of analysis would greatly increase our knowledge of past trade, travel routes, and political relationships.

The existing SAJH collections are well suited for any of these types of research because of the excellent documentation concerning provenience and excavation methods associated with the materials and the available quantity for destructive analysis. However, the lack of information consolidated in ICMS or in any other form makes it difficult to present the possibility for research to students interested in shell middens or the northwest coast.

A Broad Strategy for Improvements to Archeological Information

A number of SAJH archeology collection issues concerning consistent and proper artifact processing, reliable artifact descriptions, and accessible data are discussed in some detail in the *North Cascades National Park Service Complex & Ebey's Landing National Historical Reserve Museum Management Plan* (2005: pg. 49 - 50). Addressing these deficiencies will require a great amount of time, effort, and funding to improve the accessibility, storage, and use of the archeology collection. A clear strategy for undertaking the noted deficiencies for both the historic era and pre-contact sites is needed and can be achieved only through partnering with the Burke Museum and Fort Vancouver's Northwest Cultural Resource Institute (see Issue D). **First steps in improving the SAJH archeology collection are listed below.**

- A number of known information gaps exist for some of the materials that have been fully processed and analyzed. For instance, information from analysis completed by University of Washington researchers should be entered into ICMS. Resolving these issues is important to complete the trajectory of current research.

- The unanalyzed bone samples require immediate attention since the rough taxonomy will help to summarize the composition of faunal remains in the assemblage and will identify human remains for repatriation.

- A large number of samples are unprocessed. Sediment, shell, and rock appear to have the greatest volume in the assemblage. Much of the rock was retained for lab analysis to determine if it had been altered from fire processes. Determining the data potential for these stones is needed before these materials can be dismissed as naturally present in the site. The sediment and shell samples should be reduced in volume to a liter that is reserved for future research. Any remaining sample should be retained for a brief period as potential educational materials. For instance, geoarcheology classes may need material for teaching students how to conduct grain-size analysis. A search for interested researchers or professors would help to increase the visibility of the SAJH collection.

- Since the volume of material in the collection is large, a representative sample of the assemblage should be selected for basic analysis. For instance, cataloged items noted as bone should at least include a taxonomy descriptor (mammal, bird, etc) and stone artifacts should indicate if they are 'flakes,' 'points,' or 'fire cracked.'

- All information needs to be updated in ICMS with current copies at all SAJH repositories.

Some of this work is being undertaken by students at the University of Washington and the Burke Museum as a part of the archaeological overview and assessment. However, the cost of completing all of the needed steps for all of the material is extremely high. The Burke is uniquely situated to address the identified curation needs because the museum director and archeology collection manager retain much of the institutional memory associated with the site excavation. In order to address the identified needs for the pre-contact archeology sites, a designated fellowship between the park and the archeology division of the Burke Museum should be created. A funded program would ensure measured improvement to the pre-contact collections that need the greatest attention. Ideally the tasks associated with the fellowship would involve museology and archeology students working together on the identified tasks.

The most difficult hurdle for the types of projects discussed throughout the museum management planning effort is finding appropriate funding sources. Many of the curation and analysis tasks do not fit well with funding sources for either the Museum Management Program or the Archeology Program. Processing and analysis projects rarely rank above the funding cut-line. Thus, for processing, description and analysis projects to receive the funding needed the various tasks should be nested in other SAJH archeology or museum management projects, particularly research projects.

The historic archeology collection requires funding to address the need for more appropriate description and analysis of previously under-analyzed artifact classes. Since all of the material from the historical archeology investigations have been processed (fully cleaned, housed and properly labeled), a project statement proposing analysis and collection care improvements should be defined. A project directed solely at re-analysis will encounter the same hurdles in ranking as mentioned above yet this project could be included in a larger Hudson's Bay Company research project or as part of a multi-park interpretive effort. A research and curation strategy will have to be crafted between SAJH and FOVA to identify feasible avenues for accomplishing object descriptions and analysis.

Recommendations

- The agreement between SAJH and the Burke Museum of Natural History and Culture should be amended to include the other Burke divisions that manage SAJH collections. This agreement should identify the potential for collaborative research that will improve the usability of the collection and further our understanding of the various disciplines.

- Efforts in attracting new research should be undertaken by SAJH and PWR-Seattle employees. A plan outlining avenues to pursue in both providing researchers with the materials remaining after processing for their use and attracting new research should be completed by the consolidated call during fiscal year 2010.

- Collaboration between the NPS and the Burke is needed to create a funded fellowship directed toward improvements to the assemblages and artifact analysis.

- A detailed strategy defining the steps for processing, analysis, and re-housing materials excavated during the University of Washington Field School should be completed as part of the Archaeological Overview, Assessment and Research Design. This will require further collaboration between the NPS and SAJH.

- Oral history interviews with Julie K. Stein, Laura Phillips and Mary Parr (pre-contact component) and Rick Sprague (historic component) concerning the excavations at English Camp should be conducted and assumed into the archives.

- SAJH employees should be supported to engage with the collection and assist with the development of new exhibits and interpretive materials.

- Create a web page for the park that highlights the collection.

Figure 8 Harpoon point probably for sea mammal hunting, around 1,000 years old, SAJH

Issue D—
Collaborative Management
Of Museum Collections

Issue Statement

The park and the network have the potential to be a regional model for collaborative museum collections management.

Background

The museum collections from San Juan are housed at several different repositories: North Cascades National Park, Fort Vancouver National Historic Site, and numerous departments of the Burke Museum (see Table 2, page 48). The repositories were chosen both by geographical location and thematic specialty, and a variety of formal and informal agreements govern the partnerships. The overall professional management of these dispersed collections has depended on a curator-of-record who is an employee of North Cascades, supported in part by funding from San Juan's base budget under an annual memorandum of agreement.

The Burke Museum curates all pre-contact archeological artifacts from the park (with the exception of some minimally processed materials from field school excavations) and their associated records. In addition, vascular plant samples are held in the herbarium and a small number of paleontological and biological specimens are housed in different departments of the museum. All of the collections at the Burke are on loan; the loan agreements are renewed regularly by the curator-of-record and although a memorandum of understanding with the Archeology Department exists and will not expire until 2010, no more detailed agreements exist with other departments.

The majority of archival materials and historic-era archeological artifacts are curated in the North Cascades facility, with the exception of the archeological collection from the Belle Vue Sheep Farm site curated at Fort Vancouver. This Hudson's Bay Company collection was loaned to Fort Vancouver in support of a mission to create a fur trade research center at that park, an arrangement brokered by the regional curator. A memorandum of understanding between San Juan and Fort Vancouver was signed in 1995. Three years later, a memorandum of agreement that requested funding for further analysis of the collection was signed but never implemented by either park, according to the former FOVA curator. With subsequent staff changeover, much of the original, assumedly verbal communication surrounding the partnership between San Juan and Fort Vancouver has been lost.

Discussion

As a small cultural park with museum collections stored elsewhere, San Juan is in a position that will become increasingly common. The National Park Service's recent curation facility plan, *Park Museum Collection Storage Plan* (2007), reflects a trend to consolidate museum collections of all kinds in fewer repositories. While this may be more cost-effective, park staff may have difficulty accessing the collection as a resource for interpretive programs and baseline data; visitors and researchers face additional travel and coordination with another park unit; and the powerful connection between authentic objects and their original physical context is compromised. Information, funds, and tangible items must move not only between divisions, but between parks. It is easy to allow a museum collection to languish, underutilized by both park staff and the researchers they host. Yet the obstacles are not insurmountable. With increased communication, creative use of technology, and shared expertise, an offsite museum collection can remain one of a park's primary resources. Artifacts, natural history specimens, and historic items are essential aspects of the national significance of a site, and their tie to the park can and must be sustained.

Earlier chapters in this plan discussed some of the difficulties faced by San Juan Island NHP because of this arrangement, and offered ideas for mitigating these challenges and moving forward. The theme that underlies each section is that it is impossible to discuss the park in a museum context without also looking at the operations of at least three other entities. This section of the plan focuses on San Juan Island NHP's opportunities within a wider National Park Service context, specifically how the park can leverage its membership in the North Coast and Cascades Network to further the staff's goals with regard to collections access and use. Indeed, the park is ideally placed for promoting strategic planning that looks at museum collections and museum staff in a novel way, and places a high value on network cooperation.

For adequate staffing and funding, the North Coast and Cascades Network must take an aggressive approach to long-range museum planning and support. This MMP team suggests that the most appropriate route is based on increased collaboration between parks. The network has several journeyman-level curators, and they each have unique areas of emphasis on which their colleagues could capitalize. In addition, new cultural resource positions could be hired as shared employees through network base and project funding requests, to most cost-effectively achieve a professional museum management program *across* the network. Consolidation at a centralized facility, one that is accessible to researchers, should be seriously considered. These are not new ideas; many of them are echoed in existing museum management plans for other parks, as well as in the Servicewide curation facility plan. The planning effort at San Juan Island NHP, however, highlighted the urgency of this need and provides a perfect case study for approaching curation as a joint endeavor.

Reducing the number of facilities which curate San Juan museum items would make management of the collection more efficient and coordination between the park and the curator-of-record more streamlined. The pre-contact and natural history collections at the Burke Museum are heavily used by researchers, and they are currently curated free of charge; it makes sense to have this segment of the collection remain there for the foreseeable future. The remainder of the collection could be consolidated at a proposed new facility at Fort Vancouver. Though physically farther from San Juan Island than North Cascades, there are several advantages to housing the collections there. First, the sites are tied by many historic themes, namely the Hudson's Bay Company corporate and agricultural activities, and the flow of U.S. Army personnel between Vancouver Barracks and the Island. Second, Fort Vancouver cultural resources staff have specific expertise in archeological collections of the fur trade and early Army eras, and analysis of the collection would be improved. Third, the park's research center function and urban location mean increased accessibility to and interpretation of the collection for researchers and the general public.

With a collection that is stored elsewhere and a curator-of-record that is an employee of another unit, museum operations become more complex and more dependent on the involvement of a park's superintendent and chiefs. This is the level at which agreements between parks must be formalized and periodically revised (preferably through face-to-face meetings) to draw upon the diverse talents available at each park and crystallize joint efforts.

Many of the recommendations below, while generally germane to staff with museum management responsibilities, are addressed to upper level staff. When a park depends on the services of a curator-of-record, basic accountability and preservation will be achieved. However, key staff members at a park have the responsibility to assist in promoting the *use* of a collection—several specific and relatively inexpensive methods are recommended below—and reminding their employees, visitors, and local community that the museum collection is an invaluable part of the site they preserve.

Since SAJH's collections are located elsewhere, the park needs to provide information about those materials and where they are located. Developing small publications, such as park brochures and collections fact sheets (see Appendix G) would aid in providing information to the public and park staff about the collections, where they are located, and how to access them.

Recommendations

- Consolidate collections at the new curation facility at Fort Vancouver when completed, with the exception of items currently housed at the Burke Museum.

- Initiate formal agreements between partners, with clear strategies for encouraging information flow and financial support, detailed descriptions of projects, and recurring reporting dates. Periodically review and revise agreements with partners.

- Commit to regular face-to-face meetings between partners as well as tours of collection facilities to view new accessions.

- Consult with the curator-of-record, early and often, whenever a project is planned that will result in a collection of objects or archival materials.

- Develop a fact sheet for visitors and researchers that describes the museum resources of the park, their location(s), and the process for accessing them.

- Support technology-based applications for sharing collection data both between parks and with visitors.

- Incorporate museum resources at the site whenever possible, through exhibit development, educational or outreach programs based on material culture, and support for student projects.

- Proactively develop and support Cultural Resources OFS and PMIS requests which enhance cooperative work between parks.

- Coordinate with the regional curator and the board of directors to sponsor a network-wide discussion of museum issues, where "best practices" for addressing the management of offsite collections can be evaluated and shared among parks.

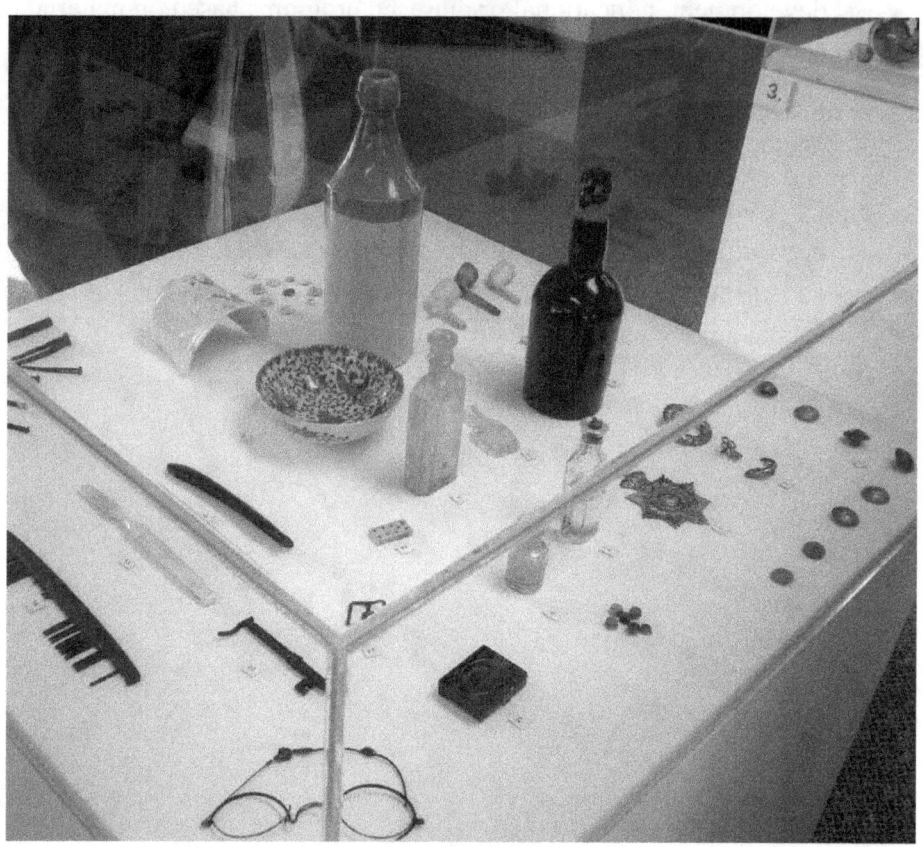

Figure 9   Exhibit case, American Camp Visitor Center, SAJH

San Juan Island National Historical Park Museum Management Plan

Good museum management planning requires an understanding of the library, archives, and museum collection resources as they currently exist, background on how and why these resources were developed, and information on what is required to preserve the resources and make them available for use. To be effective, planners must first review park-specific documentation such as reports, checklists, and plans, then make recommendations based on professional theory and techniques that are documented in the professional literature.

This bibliography lists the park-specific materials used in developing the San Juan Island National Historical Park Museum Management Plan.

Anderson, Phoebe S. Unpublished data on nutritional value of shellfish. 2007.

Bathurst, Ronda R. "Archaeological Evidence of Intestinal Parasites from Coastal Shell Middens." *Journal of Archaeological Science*, Vol. 32, 2005, pp. 115-123.

Bawaya, M. "Archaeology: Curation in Crisis." *Science*, Vol. 317, 24 August 2007, pp. 1025-1026.

Bayless, Jonathan, Robert Applegate, Kelly Cahill, Kirstie Haertel, and Diane Nicholson. *North Cascades National Park Service Complex and Ebey's Landing National Historical Reserve Museum Management Plan*. Seattle, WA: Department of the Interior, National Park Service, Pacific West Region, 2005.

Bohnert, Allen. *Fort Vancouver National Historic Site Museum Management Plan Addendum*. Vancouver, WA: Fort Vancouver National Historic Site, 2010.

Boxberger, Daniel L. *San Juan Island Cultural Affiliation Study*. Seattle, WA: National Park Service, Pacific Northwest Region, ca. 1992.

Cannon, Kelly June. *San Juan Island National Historical Park Administrative History*. Seattle, WA: National Park Service, Seattle Support Office, 1997.

Close, Angela. *Finding the People Who Flaked the Stone at English Camp (San Juan Island)*. Salt Lake City, UT: University of Utah Press, 2006.

Deo, Jennie N., J.O. Stone, and J.K. Stein. "Building Confidence in Shell: Variations in the Marine Radiocarbon Reservoir Correction for the Northwest Coast over the Past 3,000 Years," *American Antiquity*, Vol. 69, No. 4, October, 2004, pp. 771-786.

Daniels, Phobe S. "A Gendered Model of Pre-contact Resource Depression: A Case Study on the Northwest Coast of North America." Doctoral Dissertation, Seattle: University of Washington, 2009.

Erigero, Patricia, and Barry Schnoll. *Crook House Historic Structures Report, English Camp, San Juan Island National Historical Park, San Juan Island, Washington*. Seattle, WA: National Park Service, Pacific Northwest Region, Cultural Resources Division, 1984.

Fuller, Tamsen. *Conservation Survey and Assessment Report for the Archeological Collections of San Juan Island National Historical Park*. Corvallis, OR: Northwest Object Conservation, 1998.

Hoddenbach Consulting. *Integrated Pest Management Plan for Museum Storage in North Cascades National Park*. Marblemount, WA: National Park Service, 2001.

Kotler, Neil and Philip Kotler, Wendy I. Kotler. *Museum Strategy and Marketing: Designing Missions, Building Audiences, Generating Revenue and Resources*. San Francisco: Jossey-Bass Inc., 1999.

Lawton, Alva. *Moss Flora of the Pacific Northwest*. Nichinan: The Hattori Botanical Laboratory, 1971.

Lentz, Florence K. with Dr. William Woodward and Bridget E.J. Spiers. *Historic Furnishings Report: British Camp Hospital, San Juan Island National Historical Park, San Juan Island, Washington*. Seattle, WA: Department of the Interior, National Park Service, Pacific Northwest Region, Cultural Resources Division, 1990.

McKenzie, R. "Parasite Findings in Archeological Remains: Diagnosis and Interpretation." *Quaternary International,* Vol. 180:1, 2008, pp. 17 – 21.

National Park Service. *Curatorial Facilities Strategy.* Seattle, WA: National Park Service, Pacific West Region, Cultural Resources, 2006.

_____. Marblemount Curation Facility Collection Management Protocols. Marblemount, WA: National Park Service, nd.

_____. *Park Museum Collection Storage Plan.* Washington, DC: National Park Service, Park Museum Management Program, 2007.

_____. *San Juan Island N.H.P. Interpretive Prospectus.* Harpers Ferry, WV: National Park Service, Harpers Ferry Center, Division of Interpretive Planning, 1984.

_____. *San Juan Island National Historical Park Final General Management Plan and Environmental Impact Statement.* Seattle, WA: Department of the Interior, National Park Service, Pacific West Region, 2008.

Pyle, Robert Michael. *The Butterflies of Cascadia: A Field Guide to all the Species of Washington, Oregon and Surrounding Territories.* Seattle Audubon Society, 2002.

Sprague, Roderick, ed. *San Juan Archeology: Volume I.* Moscow, ID: University of Idaho, 1983.

_____. *San Juan Archeology: Volume II.* Moscow, ID: University of Idaho, 1983.

Stein, Julie K, ed. *Deciphering A Shell Midden.* San Diego: Academic Press, Inc., 1992.

Stein, Julie K, ed. *Exploring Coast Salish Prehistory: The Archeology of San Juan Island.* Seattle: University of Washington Press, 2000.

Stein, Julie K., Jennie N. Deo, Laura S. Phillips. "Big Sites - Short Time: Accumulation Rates in Archeological Sites," *Journal of Archaeological Science* Vol. 30, 2003, pp. 297-316.

Thompson, Erwin N. *Historic Resource Study, San Juan Island National Historical Park, Washington.* Denver, CO: U.S. Department of the Interior, National Park Service, Denver Service Center, 1972.

Vouri, Michael P. *The Pig War: Standoff on Griffin Bay.* Friday Harbor, WA: Griffin Bay Books,1999.

_____. Outpost of Empire: *The Royal Marines and the Joint Occupation of San Juan Island.* Seattle: Northwest Interpretive Association/University of Washington Press, 2004.

_____. *The Pig War.* San Francisco: Arcadia Publishing, 2008.

Appendix A—
Letter of Agreement Concerning
Museum Collections Management
for Fiscal Year 2009

United States Department of the Interior
NATIONAL PARK SERVICE
San Juan Island National Historical Park
P.O. Box 429
Friday Harbor, WA 98250

IN REPLY REFER TO: H20 (SAJH)

October 16, 2009

To: Superintendent, North Cascades National Park Service
           Complex

From: Superintendent, San Juan Island National Historical Park

Subject: Letter of Agreement Concerning Museum Collections
           Management for Fiscal Year 2009

The purpose of this Letter of Agreement (hereinafter referred to as LA) is to
provide, in the most cost-efficient and effective manner, for the necessary and
required accountability, storage, and treatment of cultural and scientific
collections recovered from San Juan Island National Historical Park.

Purpose and Need

As park managers of National Park Service units, we recognize our
responsibility for the systematic identification, testing, recording, and
preservation of park resources, as well as the preservation of objects, specimens,
and associated data under various Federal Laws and regulations. This includes,
but is not limited to: Act for the Preservation of American Antiquities (34
STAT. 255); Historic Sites Act of 1935 (49 STAT. 666); Museum Act of 1955
(69 STAT. 242); Archeological Resources Protection Act of 1979; Title 36,

Code of Federal Regulations Part 79, Curation of Federally-Owned and Administered Archeological Collections; and Title 36, Code of Federal Regulations, Sec. 2.5. This responsibility also applies to the cataloging, preservation, and storage of recovered data and material under these Federal Laws as well as the following NPS Director's Orders and Staff Directive: *Director's Order #24*: *Museum Collections Management; Director's Order # 26: Projects Must Fund Basic Preservation of Museum Collections They Generate;* and *Staff Directive 96-1*: *Linking Cultural and Natural Resource and Socio-economic Data to Park Planning and Management.*

San Juan Island National Historical Park does not have a curatorial facility or staff to manage its collection of over 1,000,000 museum objects. These objects are managed on its behalf at North Cascades National Park Service Complex, the Burke Museum, University of Washington; and Fort Vancouver National Historic Site. North Cascades National Park Service Complex has a museum curation facility at Marblemount, Washington within relatively close proximity to San Juan Island National Historical Park, but has only partial funding for a museum curator. San Juan Island National Historical Park also provides partial funding for the museum curator position.

Beginning in FY 2003, all projects involving museum collections must be supervised by a journeyman-level Curator (GS-1015-11) if they are to receive project funds through the museum management program. All accession and catalog work must be done by at least a GS-1015-09. Any employee under a GS-09 involved with any type of museum work will require daily supervision by a journeyman-level curator. Therefore, this LA is mutually beneficial by providing museum curation space and technical expertise in an efficient and cost-effective manner.

The superintendents of North Cascades National Park Service Complex (hereinafter referred to as NOCA) and San Juan Island National Historical Park (hereinafter referred to as SAJH) have signature authority to enter into agreements with other park units regarding park resource management. (*Director's Order #20: Federal Assistance and Interagency Agreements,* Chapter 4, page 1)

Park Collection Accountability

Under this LA, NOCA agrees to:

A. Provide a qualified Museum Curator (GS-1015-11), who will function as SAJH curator-of-record, to catalog, preserve, and generally manage the SAJH collection according to an approved annual work plan (Attachment A), and reflect this workload in at least one critical element in that person's performance standards. NOCA also agrees to solicit from the SAJH chief of resource management an informal appraisal of the museum curator's collection management performance prior to completing mid-year progress reviews and the end-of-the-year performance evaluation.

B. Designate the above NOCA museum curator as the liaison with the SAJH chief of resource management for all matters relating to the SAJH museum collection.

Under this LA, SAJH agrees to:

Cover the expenses for the NOCA museum curator to preserve and manage the SAJH collection in conjunction with a mutually-approved annual work plan. This will be accomplished through a transfer of funds for at least $13,000 for FY 2009. These funds will be used for the curator's salary costs, to purchase technical support for ANCS+ as required by federal contract, and to support collection management activities associated with cataloging and the ANCS+ program. Of the above-mentioned funds, $1,500 will be dedicated to purchasing ANCS+ support for SAJH collections management or for the Burke Museum archeology collections management.

Park Collection Management

Under this LA, NOCA agrees to:

Allow the SAJH superintendent, or his designated curatorial representative(s), with sufficient advance notice to inspect all or any part of the SAJH museum collection maintained by NOCA and make objects in that collection available to SAJH for exhibitions.

Under this LA, SAJH agrees to:

Coordinate all mutually agreed upon collection management activities with the NOCA supervisor of the Cultural Resources Work Group.

General Provisions

SAJH and NOCA mutually agree to the following:

All work assignments will be made through and with the approval of the NOCA supervisor of the Cultural Resources Work Group.

Terms of LA

The term of this LA is one (1) fiscal year. The parties will jointly review the results of this LA at the end of each fiscal year. The LA may be amended at any time by the written mutual consent of the parties, and the approved amendments will immediately become part of the LA.

Key Officials

A. North Cascades National Park Service Complex:

Palmer Jenkins, Superintendent

B. San Juan Island National Historical Park:

Peter Dederich, Superintendent

Termination
This LA may be terminated by either party by providing sixty (60) days written notice to the other party.

North Cascades National Park Service Complex
810 State Route 20
Sedro-Woolley, WA   98284

Palmer Jenkins, Superintendent   Date

San Juan Island National Historical Park
P.O. Box 429
Friday Harbor, WA   98250

Peter Dederich, Superintendent   Date

Attachment A

Museum Collection Background

The North Cascades National Park Service Complex (NOCA) museum curator is the designated curator-of-record for the museum collections of both NOCA and San Juan Island National Historic Park (SAJH). Funds are transferred annually from SAJH to NOCA to support collections management for the SAJH collection. The NOCA collection is estimated at over 210,000 catalogued objects (not including backlog), and the SAJH collection is estimated to contain over 838,000 catalogued objects (not including backlog). About one-third of the SAJH collections are housed at the NOCA Marblemount Curation Facility. Two-thirds are housed at the Burke Museum, University of Washington in Seattle, Washington. A collection of 5,000 objects is housed at Fort Vancouver National Historic Site. SAJH has historic and pre-contact archeological objects on display at the American Camp visitor center near Friday Harbor, Washington.

Current Museum Collection Management Support for FY 09

For FY 09, NOCA will provide $43,000 (13 pay periods) of support to manage the NOCA collection, and SAJH will provide $13,000 (4 pay periods salary) of support to manage the SAJH collection. The Marblemount Curation Facility currently provides equipment for environmental monitoring and archival indexing, including an environmental datalogger for SAJH curatorial storage, document scanner, slide scanner, digital camera, and laptop computer. Curator personnel costs in FY 09 are anticipated to be $3,252/PP, and benefits paid during furlough are presently calculated at $750 per pay period.

Funded SAJH Museum Collection Management Activities for FY 09

The condition of the SAJH database in ANCS+ is presently evaluated by the museum curator as good on a scale of poor-fair-good-excellent. The initial emphasis of the SAJH collection management activities for FY 09 will be to provide a secure, data quality-assured logical database foundation by addressing identified problems and inconsistencies in the SAJH collection database. Additional activities will be directed to establishing a systematic management approach for the SAJH museum collection and its managing partners.

Administrative Management Activities to be Accomplished in FY 09 (4 pay periods)

Burke – insure data updates accuracy	2 weeks
1. Construct and submit NPS Museum Management Reports	1 week
2. Maintain and develop, in consultation, letters of agreement, loans maintained as current	2 weeks
3. Fiscal budgeting and payroll, PMIS proposal development	1/2 week
4. Collection housekeeping and monitoring	1 week
5. Collection access and response to research requests	1/2 week
6. Archival finding-aid database development	1 week

NOCA-funded Shared Collection Management Activities at Marblemount Curation Facility (2 pay periods)

Planning efforts to update Scope of Collections Statement, Emergency Operations, Housekeeping, Integrated Pest Management, Security/fire, IT and digital data

Museum Collection Protection and Preservation Program (MCPPP)-funded collection management activities at Marblemount Curation Facility, San Juan Island NHP, and the Burke Museum, Seattle, Washington (3 pay periods)

Identify museum management issues facing the park, and present recommendations to address these issues.

Discussion among planning team, park management, and staff to cooperatively develop a museum management plan which recommends actions designed to develop collections management and access.

Appendix B—
Memorandum of Understanding

Between
San Juan Island National Historical Park
And
The Burke Museum of Natural History and Culture
Archeology Section

The purpose of this Memorandum of Understanding (MOU) is to provide the necessary and required accountability, storage, and treatment of cultural and scientific collections recovered from San Juan Island National Historical Park (SAJH).

The National Park Service has specific responsibilities for the systematic identification, testing, recording, and preservation of park resources and the preservation of objects, specimens, and associated data under various Federal Laws and regulations. These include, but are not limited to: Act for the Preservation of American Antiquities (34 STAT. 255); Historic Sites Act of 1935 (49 STAT. 666); Museum Act of 1955 (69 STAT. 242); Archeological Resources Protection Act of 1979; Title 36, Code of Federal Regulations Part 79, Curation of Federally-Owned and Administered Archeological Collections; and Title 36, Code of Federal Regulations, Sec. 2.5. This responsibility also applies to the cataloging, preservation, and storage of recovered data and material under these federal laws (*Director's Order #24: Museum Collections Management*).

San Juan Island National Historical Park does not have a curatorial facility or staff to manage its collection of approximately 840,000 museum objects (according to the 2006 Collections Management Report). Certain portions of this collection are at the Burke Museum, which has been providing primary care for those collections for a number of years. During the years of continuing excavation at the park, this care was provided as part of a series of cooperative agreements between the park and the museum. The most recent of these agreements expired in 1996, and it has not been replaced with a formal agreement or other documentation authorizing the museum to manage the park collections.

The superintendent of San Juan Island National Historical Park has signature authority to enter into agreements with non-profit organizations such as the museum regarding park resource management (*Director's Order #20: Agreements* and NPS Agreements Handbook, Chapter 9, "Responsibilities," p. 209. See: http://www.nps.gov/hfc/acquisition/agreements.htm. This MOU will be mutually beneficial to both parties in that it will allow uninterrupted management of the material at the museum. Furthermore, this agreement does not commit the NPS to providing financial assistance in any form, such as furnishing NPS property, goods, or services.

The following general conditions apply:

Point of contact for the National Park Service is the superintendent of San Juan Island National Historical Park. Point of contact for the Burke Museum of Natural History and Culture is its curator of archeology. All official information will flow between these two entities with copies to the NPS regional curator – Oakland and NPS regional archeologist – Seattle. Day-to-day work and communication will flow between the curator-of-record for SAJH and the Burke archeology collections manager. In addition, the NPS regional archeologist – Seattle will provide oversight on questions regarding archeology and will respond in the absence of the SAJH curator-of-record to issues needing immediate resolution.

NPS museum collections will be managed to meet NPS museum standards contained in *DO#24: Museum Collections Management* (see: http://www.nps.gov/policy/DOrders/DOrder24.html and the NPS *Museum Handbook* http://www.cr.nps.gov/museum/publications/index.htm as well as 36 CFR Part 79, Curation of Federally-Owned and Administered Archeological Collections: http://www.cr.nps.gov/aad/tools/36cfr79.htm

There will be no outgoing loan agreements for the SAJH collections from the Burke Museum. All such requests will be forwarded to the SAJH superintendent and curator who will complete all appropriate paperwork, if it is decided to approve such loans from the SAJH collections. On-campus research and related loans will be approved by the Burke curator of archeology and reported in the subsequent annual report.

If previously unrecognized NAGPRA-related objects are identified in the SAJH collections stored at the Burke Museum, Burke archeology staff will immediately inform the SAJH superintendent who will contact the appropriate NPS staff for guidance, particularly the regional NPS NAGPRA coordinator. The NPS will be solely responsible for any consultation or other actions under NAGPRA.

Burke Museum Archeology Section will document all use of SAJH collections stored at the Burke Museum and maintain records of such use. These data will be included in the annual reports to the SAJH superintendent. Such use includes, but is not limited to, educational use by university instructors, research by graduate students and professors, exhibitions, and so on.

All on-site research use of the collections will be documented by use of the Burke Museum Research Request Form – Archeology Section (Exhibit 1). The Burke Museum curator of archeology will approve these research requests. If the curator determines that the proposed research request is not appropriate, s/he will inform the SAJH superintendent in case there is any potential controversy surrounding such a decision. Copies of the Research Request Form and attached documentation, such as a research design, will be appended to the annual report to be sent to the park. Two (2) copies of all reports and/or publications derived from this research will be forwarded to SAJH for inclusion in the park library and archives (currently located at the North Cascades museum facility at Marblemount). The NPS will also provide copies of any reports, publications, or other information generated about the collections to the Burke Museum.

All removal of collections from the Burke Museum to other facilities at the University of Washington will be documented by the Burke Museum Loan Agreement (Exhibit 2) approved by the Burke Museum curator of archeology and signed by the borrower. If materials from the loan are moved at different times from the museum, they will be documented on a Burke Museum Invoice of Specimens form (Exhibit 3), which is countersigned by the borrower and the Burke Museum archeology collections manager. Copies of these documents will be appended to the annual report to be sent to the park. Two (2) copies of all reports and/or publications from this research will be forwarded to SAJH for inclusion in the park library and archives.

Removal of materials from collections will be documented with a Burke Museum Temporary Removal Slip placed in the objects' locations, and will include catalog number, provenience numbers, object name, location, temporary location, removed by, date removed, and so on.

Requests for copies of photographs from field records will be documented by the Burke Museum Archeology Section Photograph Request Form (Exhibit 4) with the following credit line appended: "please credit: National Park Service, San Juan Island National Historical Park, catalog number SAJH _____. Materials currently located at the Burke Museum of Natural History and Culture." One copy of the publication will be forwarded to SAJH for inclusion in the park archives or library. Copies of these documents will be appended to the annual report to be sent to the park. Because these images are in the public domain, no use-fee may be charged for the photographs although the Burke Museum may recover any costs associated with duplication.

All requests for destructive analysis will be forwarded to the SAJH superintendent by the Research and Permit Reporting System process. This system will address appropriate peer review on an individual permit application basis. The NPS must approve all such uses as outlined in *DO#28: Cultural Resource Management.* http://www.nps.gov/policy/DOrders/DOrder28.html and *NPS-28: Cultural Resource Management Guideline* http://www.nps.gov/history/history/online_books/nps28/28contents.htm

All conservation needs will be forwarded to the SAJH superintendent for consideration.

As additional research on the collection occurs, the SAJH catalog database will be updated with this information. The SAJH curator will review for consistency with NPS standards and policies prior to appending to the SAJH master database.

The Burke Museum archeology collections manager and SAJH curator will consult about researcher guidance presented verbally to researchers by Burke Museum staff. Although information may need to be tailored to individual researchers, it is recommended that some general guidance for using SAJH collections in the future should be drafted in partnership and provided in written form.

Reporting

- At least twice each year, the SAJH curator-of-record will visit the Burke Museum to work with the staff on issues and to complete data transfer of the ANCS+ database between the museum and the park.

- On an annual basis (due by September 1 each year), the Burke Museum will provide a report to the superintendent of San Juan Island National Historical Park with copies to the SAJH curator-of-record, the regional curator, and the regional archeologist with the following information, based upon activity during the year:

- Copies of Research Request Form(s) – Archeology Section

- Copies of Loan Agreement(s) for internal University of Washington use of the collections outside of the Burke Museum

- Copies of Photograph Request Form(s)

- Copy of the SAJH database (if changes have been made to the database in the year)

- Statistics on numbers of users of the collections

- Annually by August 15, each park must complete an inventory of museum property. The SAJH curator will generate the random sample for the SAJH collection. If any items located at the Burke Museum are included, the SAJH superintendent will send the Burke Museum curator of archeology a list of the item(s) to be physically inventoried by June 1 of each year. This list will include catalog number, object name, and object location (which will include provenience information). The Burke Museum archeology collections manager will physically locate each item. The curator of archeology will certify in writing to the SAJH superintendent that the items are all present and accounted for by July 15 each year. The SAJH curator will conduct spot checks during visits to the Burke Museum as an additional point of accountability. If any item is determined lost, the Burke Museum curator of archeology will immediately inform the SAJH superintendent, who will initiate an appropriate investigation in conjunction with the Burke Museum staff.

National Park Service will provide:

- Copies of the latest version of ANCS+. NPS will load ANCS+ and subsequent upgrades onto a Burke Museum Archeology Section computer that will be considered a workstation for the SAJH annual support request to ReDiscovery (museum catalog software company).

- A current copy of the SAJH catalog database for the collections with materials located at the Burke Museum (Accession # SAJH-00005; -00007; -00015; -00021; -00025; -00026; -00031; -00032; -00039; -00040; -00041; -00042; -00046; -00055; -00057; -00058; -00059; -00075; -00091)

- Copy(ies) of conservation report(s) that have been completed for any of the collections located at the Burke Museum

- *Museum Handbook*, Parts I, II, and III

- Museum storage equipment which will be labeled as NPS property (as funding allows)

- Copies of any reports or other documents related to the SAJH archeological collections located at the Burke Museum

- Within three months of receiving the annual report, the NPS will provide feedback if concerns or issues arise.

The Burke Museum will provide:

- Computer equipment with appropriate security to load ANCS+ and the SAJH database

- Appropriate personnel to manage SAJH collections

- Re-housing supplies for minor collections storage maintenance

- Copies of any reports or other documents related to the SAJH archeological collections located at the Burke Museum

The Burke Museum and the National Park Service agree to work together to preserve, protect, and make accessible these important collections.

Working through the Pacific Northwest Cooperative Ecosystem Studies Unit (PNW CESU), whose host campus is the University of Washington, the NPS may undertake additional projects in collaboration with the Burke Museum, as time and funds permit. The CESU agreement allows for cooperative projects between federal agencies and universities in the areas of research, education, and technical assistance.

The term of this MOU is three (3) years, and will terminate on October 31, 2010. The parties may jointly review the results of this MOU at the end of that period, and extend the MOU for an additional period of 90 days if necessary and desirable to both parties.

Key Officials

A. Peter Dederich

Superintendent, San Juan Island National Historical Park:

B. Peter Lape

Curator of Archeology, Burke Museum of Natural History and Culture

Termination

This MOU may be terminated by either party by providing thirty (30) days written notice to the other party.

Peter Dederich	10/24/07	Peter Lape	10/25/07
Superintendent	Date	Curator of Archeology	Date
San Juan Island National Historical Park		The Burke Museum of Natural History and Culture	

Appendix C—
Memorandum of Understanding and Memorandum of Agreement with Fort Vancouver National Historic Site

Memorandum of Understanding
Between
San Juan Island National Historical Park
And
Fort Vancouver National Historic Site

I. Background

A. Purpose

The purpose of this Memorandum of Understanding (hereinafter "MOU") is to provide necessary and required accountability, storage. and treatment of cultural and scientific collections recovered from San Juan Island National Historical Park.

B. Authority

The National Park Service is responsible for the systematic identification, testing, recording, and preservation of park resources, and the preservation of objects, specimens, and associated data under various federal laws and regulations, including the Act for the Preservation of American Antiquities (34 STAT. 255); Historic Sites Act of 1935 (49 STAT. 666); Museum Act of 1955 (69 STAT. 242); Archeological Resources Protection Act of 1979; Title 36, Code of Federal Regulations Part 79, Curation of Federally-Owned and Administered Archeological Collections; and Title 36, Code of Federal Regulations, Sec. 2.5. NPS is responsible for the cataloging, preservation, and storage of recovered data and material under these federal laws as well as

Service standards: *NPS-28: Cultural Resource Management Guideline*, Chapter 2, pp 10-12; and the NPS *Museum Handbook*.

The superintendent of Fort Vancouver National Historic Site (hereinafter referred to as FOVA) has signature authority to enter into agreements with other park units regarding park resource management.

The superintendent of San Juan Island National Historical Park (hereinafter referred to as SAJH) has signature authority to enter into agreements with other park units regarding park resource management.

II. Statement of Work

Park Collection Accountability

FOVA agrees to:

Designate one permanent staff member, by critical element in that individual's annual evaluation, as liaison with the SAJH collections manager for all matters relating to FOVA-maintained portions of the SAJH collection.

Maintain computerized catalog records (plus hard copies, if necessary) for those SAJH collections maintained at the FOVA Museum Collections Management Facility.

Prepare necessary collection management documents, such as the Annual Inventory of Museum Property, and the Annual Collection Management Report, for those collections maintained at the FOVA Museum Collections Management Facility; transmit these reports to SAJH for the review and signature of the SAJH superintendent.

SAJH agrees to:

Maintain the accession book, accession file, and working copies of the catalog record cards for the SAJH collection.

Honor budget assessments of up to $500.00 annually from FOVA against accounts identified by the SAJH superintendent for collection accountability work.

Park Collection Management

FOVA agrees to:

Provide safe, secure storage for the collection covered in this agreement, including all associated records and manuscripts. This will include providing physical access to the archeological collection and its associated records by authorized researchers upon sufficient advance notice.

Assist the SAJH superintendent with the required and necessary collection management documentation, planning, and development (i.e., the preparation of RMP Statements, 10-237s, 10-238s).

Allow the SAJH superintendent, or his designated curatorial representative(s), with sufficient advance notice to inspect all or any part of the SAJH museum collection maintained by FOVA and make objects in that collection available to SAJH for exhibitions.

SAJH agrees to:

Coordinate all mutually agreed upon collection management activities with the FOVA superintendent.

Reimburse FOVA for all agreed upon expenses associated with collection management activities.

General Provisions

SAJH and FOVA **mutually agree** to the following:

All work assignments will be made through and with the approval of the FOVA superintendent.

All reimbursement charges will be made through and with the approval of the SAJH superintendent.

Agreement Evaluation

The parties will jointly review the results of this MOU at the end of each calendar year. The MOU may be amended at any time by the written mutual consent of the parties, and the approved amendments will immediately become part of this MOU.

III. Term of the MOU

The term of the MOU is five (5) years, commencing upon the date of signature of the final signatory party to the MOU.

IV. Key Officials

A. The FOVA superintendent has the responsibility and authority for managing the MOU on behalf of that park unit.

B. The SAJH superintendent has the responsibility and authority for managing the MOU on behalf of that park unit.

V. Reports

Each party is responsible for its respective timekeeping and other required records and reports.

VI. Termination

This MOU may be terminated by either party by providing sixty (60) days written notice to the other party.

VII. Required Clauses

A. No member or delegate to Congress, or resident Commissioner, shall be admitted to any share or part of this agreement, or to any benefit that may arise therefrom, but this provision shall not be construed to extend to this agreement if made with a corporation for its general benefit.

B. During the performance of this agreement, the participants agree to abide by the terms of Executive Order 11246 on nondiscrimination against any person because of race, color, religion, sex or national origin. he participants will take affirmative action to ensure that applicants are employed without regard to their race, color, religion, sex, or national origin.

Fort Vancouver National Historic Site

612 E. Reserve Street

Vancouver, WA 08661

/s/ Dianne Cooper   8/28/95

Superintendent   Date

San Juan Island National Historical Park

P.O. Box 429

Friday Harbor, WA 98250

/s/ Robert E. Scott   9/7/95

Superintendent   Date

kb 9/17/93

SAJH_FOVA.MOU

Memorandum of Agreement
Between
San Juan Island National Historical Park
And
Fort Vancouver National Historic Site

I. Background

A. Purpose

The purpose of this Memorandum of Agreement (MA) is to provide necessary and required accountability, storage, and treatment of collections recovered from San Juan Island National Historical Park relating to the Hudson's Bay Company.

B. Authority

The National Park Service is responsible for the systematic identification, testing, recording and preservation of park resources, and the preservation of objects, specimens and associated data under various federal laws and regulations, including the Act for the Preservation of American Antiquities (34 STAT. 255); Historic Sites Act of 1935 (49 STAT. 666); Museum Act of 1955 (69 STAT. 242); Archeological Resources Protection Act of 1979; Title 36, Code of Federal Regulations Part 79, Curation of Federally-Owned and Administered Archeological Collections; and Title 36, Code of Federal Regulations, Sec. 2.5. NPS is responsible for the cataloging, preservation, and storage of recovered data and material under these federal laws as well as Service standards: *NPS-28: Cultural Resource Management Guideline*, Chapter 2, pp 10-12; and the NPS *Museum Handbook.*

The superintendent of Fort Vancouver National Historic Site (FOVA) has signature authority to enter into agreements with other park units regarding park resource management.

The superintendent of San Juan Island National Historical Park (SAJH) has signature authority to enter into agreements with other park units regarding park resource management.

II. Statement of Work

Park Collection Accountability

FOVA agrees to:

Designate one permanent staff member as liaison with the SAJH collections manager for all matters relating to FOVA-maintained portions of the SAJH collection.

Maintain computerized catalog records (plus hard copies, if necessary) for those SAJH collections maintained at the FOVA Museum Collections Management Facility.

Prepare necessary collection management documents, such as the Annual Inventory of Museum Property, and the Annual Collection Management Report, for those collections maintained at the FOVA Museum Collections Management Facility; transmit these reports to SAJH for the review and signature of the SAJH superintendent.

SAJH agrees to:

Maintain the accession book, accession file and working copies of the catalog record cards for the SAJH collection.

Honor budget assessments of up to $500.00 annually from FOVA against accounts identified by the SAJH superintendent for collection accountability work.

Park Collection Management

FOVA agrees to:

Provide safe, secure storage for the collection covered in this agreement, including all associated records and manuscripts. This will include providing physical access to the archeological collection and its associated records by authorized researchers upon sufficient advance notice.

Assist the SAJH superintendent with the required and necessary collection management documentation, planning and development (i.e., the preparation of RMP Statements, 10-237s, 10-238s).

Allow the SAJH superintendent, or his designated curatorial representative(s), with sufficient advance notice to inspect all or any part of the SAJH museum collection maintained by FOVA and make objects in that collection available to SAJH for exhibitions.

SAJH agrees to:

Coordinate all mutually agreed upon collection management activities with the FOVA superintendent.

Reimburse FOVA for all agreed upon expenses associated with collection management activities.

General Provisions

SAJH and FOVA mutually agree to the following:

All work assignments will be made through and with the approval of the FOVA superintendent.

All reimbursement charges will be made through and with the approval of the SAJH superintendent.

Agreement Evaluation

The parties will jointly review the results of this MA at the end of each calendar year. The MA may be amended at any time by the written mutual consent of the parties. The approved amendments will immediately become part of this MA.

III. Term of the MA

The term of the MA is five (5) years, commencing upon the date of signature of the final signatory party to the MA.

IV. Key Officials

The FOVA superintendent has the responsibility and authority for managing the MA on behalf of that park unit.

The SAJH superintendent has the responsibility and authority for managing the MA on behalf of that park unit.

V. Reports

Each party is responsible for its respective timekeeping and other required records and reports.

VI. Termination

This MA may be terminated by either party by providing sixty (60) days written notice to the other party.

VII. Required Clauses

A. No member or delegate to Congress, or resident Commissioner, shall be admitted to any share or part of this agreement, or to any benefit that may arise therefrom, but this provision shall not be construed to extend to this agreement if made with a corporation for its general benefit.

B. During the performance of this agreement, the participants agree to abide by the terms of Executive Order 11246 on nondiscrimination against any person because of race, color, religion, sex, or national origin. The participants will take affirmative action to ensure that applicants are employed without regard to their race, color, religion, sex, or national origin.

Fort Vancouver National Historic Site

612 E. Reserve Street

Vancouver, WA 08661

/s/ Tony Sisto   **5/19/98**

Superintendent   Date

San Juan Island National Historical Park

P.O. Box 429

Friday Harbor, WA 98250

/s/ Robert E. Scott   5/5/98

Superintendent   Date

National Park Service

Columbia Cascade Cluster

909 First Avenue

Seattle, WA 98104

/s/not required per Beth Faudree, Contracting Officer

Date

Appendix D—
NEPA Compliance Project
Checklists

NEPA Compliance Checklist for Maintenance and Construction

Project Title: _____

Project Number: _____ PMIS Number: _____

Contractor/Implementation Supervisor: _____

Company/Agency: _____

Project Start and Completion Dates: _____

PROJECT MANAGEMENT   **C.O.R. FILES**

☐   Established by COR on project-by-project basis

CURRENT WORK

☐   Correspondence   ☐   Scoping

☐   Meeting Notes   ☐   Data Collection

☐   Schedules   ☐   Public Review & Comments

☐   Budgets & Cost Estimates   ☐   Draft Plan

☐   Task Orders & Consultant Contracts ☐   Final Plan/Staff Report/FONSI

☐   Compliance & Approvals   ☐   Alternatives Form/Design Review

☐   Documentation & Photographs   ☐   Other

☐   Other

EXISTING INFORMATION   **DESIGN**

☐   Planning Documents   ☐   Design Development & Review

☐   Historical Research Comments   ☐   Schematic Design & Review Comments

☐   Infrastructure Info/Evaluations   ☐   Construction Docs & Review

☐   Site Info/Evaluations Comments   ☐   Materials Research (break out if needed)

☐   Building Info/Evaluations

☐   Market Research & Financial Analysis ☐   Outline Specifications

☐   Agreements & Lease Documents   ☐   Specifications (break out by CSI format)

☐   Other   ☐   Other

RESEARCH & WRITING

☐   Research Materials

☐   Graphics

☐   Preliminary Drafts & Comments

☐   Final Draft & Comments

☐   Other

PLANNING

☐   Other

BIDDING & CONSTRUCTION

☐   Bids & Revised Cost Estimates

☐   Submittals (break out by CSI format)

☐   Inspection Records, Photos & Reports

☐   Change Orders

☐   Operating Manuals, Warranties

☐   Construction Close-out

☐   Post Occupancy Inspections

Date Received in RPPS/Compliance: _____

Initials: _____

NEPA Compliance Checklist for Interpretation Exhibits and Plans

Project Title:_____

Project Number: _____

PMIS Number: _____

Contractor/Implementation Supervisor: _____

Company/Agency: _____

Project Start and Completion Dates: _____

Return copy of completed checklist upon completion/close-out of project.

PROJECT MANAGEMENT
- ☐ Correspondence   (including email)
- ☐ Meeting Notes
- ☐ Schedules
- ☐ Construction Docs & Review Comments
- ☐ Task Orders & Consultant Contracts
- ☐ Documentation & Photographs
- ☐ Other

DESIGN
- ☐ Schematic Design & Review Comments
- ☐ Design Development & Review Comments
- ☐ Budgets & Cost Estimates
- ☐ Specifications (break out by CSI format)
- ☐ Alternatives Form/Design Review
- ☐ Materials Research (break out if needed)
- ☐ Outline Specifications
- ☐ Other

EXISTING INFORMATION
- ☐ Planning Documents
- ☐ Historical Research
- ☐ Infrastructure Info/Evaluations
- ☐ Site Info/Evaluations
- ☐ Building Info/Evaluations
- ☐ Other

BIDDING & CONSTRUCTION
- ☐ Inspection Records, Photos & Reports
- ☐ Construction Close-out
- ☐ Bids & Revised Cost Estimates
- ☐ Submittals
- ☐ Change Orders
- ☐ Other

RESEARCH & WRITING
- ☐ Research Materials
- ☐ Graphics
- ☐ Preliminary Drafts & Comments
- ☐ Final Draft & Comments
- ☐ Other

OBJECT CONSERVATION
- ☐ Correspondence (including email)
- ☐ Treatment Reports
- ☐ Photographs

Date Received in RPPS/Compliance: _____

Initials: _____

NEPA Compliance Checklist For Basic Section 106 Compliance (per *DO#28: Cultural Resources Management Guideline*, Chapter 5, p. 60 and Appendix P, p. 307)

Project Title: _____

Project Number: _____

PMIS Number: _____

Contractor/Principal Investigator/Implementation Supervisor:
_____

University/Company/Agency: _____

Project Start and Completion Dates: _____

Return copy of completed checklist and all paper and electronic documentation regarding decision upon compilation/close-out of project.

☐   Documentation of no-effect findings
☐   All evidence of consultation with SHPOs must be retained. Include hard copies of all electronic correspondence.
☐   "Assessment of Effect" forms
☐   Other 106 documentation
☐   Correspondence
☐   Plans
☐   Photographic images

Date Received in RPPS/Compliance: _____

Initials: _____

NEPA Compliance Checklist for Archeology
(per DO#28: Cultural Resources Management Guideline, Chapter 6, p. 86)

Project Title: _____

Project Number: _____

PMIS Number: _____

Contractor/Principal Investigator: _____

University/Company/Agency: _____

Project Start and Completion Dates: _____

Return copy of completed checklist upon completion/close-out of project. Submit completed project file with Checklist Sheet attached to project file. Artifacts and project documents to be curated at SEAC.

- ☐ Artifacts
- ☐ Copy of ARPA Permit (from SEAC)
- ☐ Field notes (Copies)
- ☐ Catalog records (to NPS standards – if over 1 cu ft. of artifacts recovered, otherwise cataloged at SEAC)
- ☐ Final report
- ☐ Maps
- ☐ Drawings
- ☐ Photographs, negatives, slides (Film based required for project documentation)
- ☐ Digital photographic images (For reference use copies only)
- ☐ Videotapes
- ☐ Remote sensing data
- ☐ Copies of contracts, change orders
- ☐ Copies of cooperative agreement
- ☐ Correspondence (including e-mail)
- ☐ Repository agreements
- ☐ Specialists' reports and analyses
- ☐ Reports and manuscripts
- ☐ Artifact inventories
- ☐ Field specimen logs
- ☐ Analytical study data
- ☐ Computer documentation and data
- ☐ Conservation treatment records
- ☐ Reports on all scientific samples lost through destructive analysis

Date Received in RPPS/Compliance: _____

Initials: _____

**NEPA Compliance Checklist for Landscapes/Cultural Landscapes
(per DO#28: Cultural Resources Management Guideline, Chapter 7, p. 111)**

Project Title: _____

Project Number: _____

PMIS Number: _____

Contractor/Principal Investigator/Implementation Supervisor:
_____

University/Company/Agency: _____

Project Start and Completion Dates:

_____

Return copy of completed checklist upon completion/close-out of project.
- ☐ All associated records
- ☐ Maps
- ☐ Plans
- ☐ Sketches
- ☐ Field notes
- ☐ Photographs, negatives, slides (Film based required for project documentation)
- ☐ Digital photographic images (For reference use copies only)
- ☐ Videotapes
- ☐ Soil or pollen analyses
- ☐ Construction files
- ☐ Copies of contracts, change orders
- ☐ Copies of cooperative agreement
- ☐ Correspondence (including e-mail)
- ☐ Cultural Landscape Report
- ☐ Other reports
- ☐ Publications
- ☐ Record of Treatment (copy; including all specifications, plans, work procedures

Date Received in RPPS/Compliance: _____

Initials: _____

NEPA Compliance Checklist for Historic Structures
(per DO#28: Cultural Resources Management Guideline, Chapter 8, p. 136)

Project Title: _____

Project Number: _____

PMIS Number: _____

Contractor/Implementation Supervisor: _____

Company/Agency: _____

Project Start and Completion Dates: _____

Return copy of completed checklist upon completion/close-out of project. Submit completed project file, with Checklist Sheet attached, to project file. Material samples to be cataloged into park museum collection.

- ☐ Material (structure) samples
- ☐ Field notes
- ☐ Photographs, negatives, slides (Film based required for project documentation
- ☐ Digital photographic images (For reference use copies only)
- ☐ Videotapes
- ☐ Copies of contracts, change orders
- ☐ Copies of cooperative agreement
- ☐ Correspondence (including e-mail)
- ☐ Construction Files (including all plans and specifications)
- ☐ Reports
- ☐ Publications

Date Received in RPPS/Compliance: _____

Initials: _____

NEPA Compliance Checklist for Ethnographic/Oral History Projects

(per DO#28: Cultural Resources Management Guideline, Chapter 10, p. 165)

Project Title: _____

Project Number: _____

PMIS Number: _____

Contractor/Principal Investigator/Implementation Supervisor:

_____

University/Company/Agency: _____

Project Start and Completion Dates: _____

Return copy of completed checklist upon completion/close-out of project. Submit completed project file, with Checklist Sheet attached, to project file.

□ (Summaries of) Field notes
□ Informed Consent Release Forms
□ Oral history audio tapes
□ Transcripts
□ Videotapes
□ Photographs
□ Copies of contracts, change orders
□ Copies of cooperative agreement
□ Correspondence (including e-mail)
□ Draft report
□ Final report
□ Publications

Date Received in RPPS/Compliance: _____

Initials: _____

NEPA Compliance Checklist for Natural Resources
(per NPS-77: Natural Resources Management Guideline, Chapter 5, p. 53)

Project Title: _____

Project Number: _____

PMIS Number: _____

Contractor/Principal Investigator/Implementation Supervisor:_____

University/Company/Agency: _____

Project Start and Completion Dates: _____

Return copy of completed checklist upon completion/close-out of project. Submit completed project file, with Checklist Sheet attached to project file. All specimens to be cataloged into museum collection, but may be deposited in non-NPS repository.

☐   Field notes (NPS staff – originals; contractors – copies)
☐   NPS Collection Permit
☐   Catalog records
☐   Daily journals
☐   Maps
☐   Drawings
☐   Photographs, negatives, slides (Film based required for project documentation
☐   Digital photographic images (For reference use copies only)
☐   Videotapes
☐   Raw data sheets
☐   Remote sensing data
☐   Copies of contracts, change orders
☐   Copies of cooperative agreement
☐   Correspondence
☐   Repository agreements
☐   Specialists' reports and analyses
☐   Reports and manuscripts
☐   Collection inventories
☐   Field catalogs
☐   Analytical study data
☐   Sound recordings
☐   Computer documentation and data
☐   Tabulations and lists
☐   Specimen preparation records
☐   Conservation treatment records
☐   Reports on all scientific samples lost through destructive analysis

Date Received in RPPS/Compliance: _____

Initials: _____

NEPA Compliance Checklist for RP & PS Project File
(per DO#12: Conservation Planning and Environmental Impact Analysis Handbook, Chapter 2-12, Administrative Record)

Project Title: _____

Project Number: _____

PMIS Number: _____

Parkway District: _____ **Parkway Section:** _____ **Mile Post:** _____

Project Start and Completion Dates: _____

- ☐ Meeting notes regarding content, issues, alternatives, etc., of EA/EIS
- ☐ Minutes of meetings of public involvement
- ☐ Letters of public involvement
- ☐ Telephone call notes of public involvement
- ☐ EA for review
- ☐ EIS for review
- ☐ Approval letter to implementing division
- ☐ Copy of contract
- ☐ Copy of cooperative agreement
- ☐ Specifications
- ☐ Plans, maps
- ☐ Close-outs
- ☐ Copy of ARPA Permit
- ☐ Copy of finding of no effect from SHPO

Date Received in RPPS/Compliance: _____

Initials: _____

Mandated Retained Records for DSC Projects

Park: _____   Package Number:_____

Project Type Information: _____

Sensitive Data Present (indicate report):_____

Contract Number: _____

Project Information Files

- ❑ Correspondence that documents decisions
- ❑ project agreements
- ❑ discussions about design changes
- ❑ meeting notes
- ❑ specifications
- ❑ cost estimates
- ❑ compliance information
- ❑ draft documents and drawings
- ❑ review process information including transmittals

Any of these documents with original signatures are the record copies. DSC/NPS is required by law to keep the record copies organized and retrievable per FOIA law 5 USC 552 and 44 USC 3301.

Contract Files

- ❑ Submittals
- ❑ samples of materials used in projects
- ❑ contracts
- ❑ specifications
- ❑ contract amendments and modifications with original signatures
- ❑ justifications for contract changes
- ❑ (contract payrolls)
- ❑ contract field files
- ❑ construction dailies
- ❑ task orders
- ❑ construction correspondence
- ❑ documentation for contract disputes

NPS technical reports

- hazardous material reports
- findings of no significant impact
- O&M manuals
- value analysis reports
- post occupancy evaluations
- public involvement documents
- concessions management plans
- general management plans
- historic structure evaluations
- new area studies
- resource management reports
- special studies
- environmental assessments, etc.

Drawings

- review copies
- bid sets
- amendments
- negotiated modifications
- as-constructed drawings ("as-builts")

Information in the project files that is protected by FOIA from release to the public, e.g. the names of sub-contractors, cost estimates prior to the contract award, cost figures after the contract is awarded, social security numbers, some compliance information including some hazmat information, location of sensitive archeological sites, etc.

Appendix E— Internet Resources for Interpretation and Collection Accessibility

Below is a short list of online resources including training, accessibility guidelines, software and tutorial resources, and examples of how these technologies can be used creatively by museums and archives.

HTML Writers Guild

http://www.hwg.org/resources/accessibility/sixprinciples.html

Thanks to Section 508, accessibility for a broad audience of abilities is not only desirable but required. Thus, accessibility has become a significant factor in deciding what online technologies are appropriate for park web pages. Accessibility issues can be hard to fix, so the best practice is to be familiar with universal design principles and incorporate them into initial project planning. The NPS offers a good section on how to incorporate these design concerns, but there is other help available as well. One such source is the HTML Writer's Guild, which offers a good introduction to the World Wide Web Consortium's Web Accessibility Project.

Resource List, AAM Media and Technology Committee www.vlib.us/aam/

The American Association of Museums maintains a resource list for small museums that includes links to free programs, tutorials, and information resources. Topics include podcasting, social networking, RSS readers, virtual tours, listservs, blogs, digital rights, and image management. This list also provides links to examples of how institutions have used these tools as well as blogs by museum professionals working in these media.

PBS Program Pages

http://www.pbs.org/search/search_programsaz.html

PBS is known for its innovative and thought-provoking websites that use a wide variety of tools to interpret material. The program pages are a rich source of ideas for new online and digital projects.

Flickr

Flickr is an online image management and sharing system that has become popular with many museums and archives because of its simplicity of function, low cost, and heavy public use. Two examples of participating institutions are the Smithsonian Institution and the Seattle Municipal Archive:
http://www.flickr.com/photos/smithsonian/

http://www.flickr.com/photos/seattlemunicipalarchives/

Southeast Archeological Center (SEAC)
http://www.nps.gov/history/seac/research.htm

Fort Vancouver Archeology and Collections

http://www.nps.gov/fova/historyculture/archaeology-and-collections-a.htm

SEAC and Fort Vancouver offer good examples of how park collection web pages are able to offer materials for both serious researchers and casual browsers. The contrast between their pages illustrates the possibilities for design that are both individualized for different parks and still meet NPS criteria.

National Park Service Archeology Program

Archeology for Interpreters
http://www.nps.gov/history/archeology/AforI/index.htm

Why Archeology Matters
http://www.nps.gov/history/archeology/IforA/index.htm

Artifact and Archive Collections at Fort Vancouver

Archeological excavations have taken place here over the last 60 years, creating a vast collection unparalleled at any other fur trade site. The collection also encompasses many artifacts of U.S. Army origin, objects which help interpret Vancouver Barracks and early military life in the area. Currently, the site curates more than two million objects, almost 200,000 of which are in the study collection.

Collections from three other National Park Service sites are also stored here: Fort Colville from Lake Roosevelt National Recreation Area, Whitman Mission National Historic Site's Fort Nez Perce, and Belle Vue Sheep Farm from San Juan National Historical Park.

The entire collection is curated in the Fur Store building at the fort site; this facility not only provides a state-of-the-art storage and climate control system for the collection, but also accommodations for researchers and a reference library.

The Northwest Cultural Resources Institute (NCRI), housed here, facilitates and supports research relating to archeology, history, and museum management. Investigations are ongoing in the park's "living laboratory," where science and stewardship go hand in hand.

Dig deeper...

- For a virtual visit to the park's collection, visit the web catalog at http://www.museum.nps.gov/fova/page.htm

- To view the collection onsite or use the reference library, make an appointment with Curator Tessa Langford at 360-816-6252 or by email at theresa_langford@nps.gov

Appendix G—
Burke Museum Forms

Archeology Section Research Request Form

On-Campus Loan Agreement

Outgoing Loan Agreement

Outgoing Research Loan Request

Invoice of Specimens

Image Reproduction Policy

Field Collection Form

Thomas Burke Memorial Washington State Museum
Box 353010, Seattle, WA 98195-3010. 206-685-3849

Archaeology Section
Research Request Form

Name:_____ Date:_____

Institutional Affiliation:_____

Address:_____

Telephone:_____ Email:_____

Nature of Research:

( ) Publication   ( ) Basic Research

( ) Exhibition   ( ) Student Research

                                                                What Class?_____

                                                                 Is it for Dissertation/Thesis?_____

Title/Publication:_____

Subject:_____

Research Sponsor/Supervisor:_____

Additional Researchers to Accompany Applicant_____

Materials Sought:

( ) Photographs   ( ) Documents

( ) Recordings   ( ) Collection Records

( ) Specimens/Artifacts   ( ) Other:_____

Requested Date(s) of Access:_____ Reviewed by:_____

( ) Approved   ( )Disapproved   Reason Disapproved_____

Supervised/Assisted by:_____

Fees Charged:_____

CONDITIONS OF ACCESS/CODE OF CONDUCT

1. Faculty, student, researcher, and public access to the Library, Archives, and storage collections is available by appointment only. Appointments must be made in advance with the Division's Collection Manager or Curators. At least two weeks' advance notice is required except under special circumstances since appointments are scheduled as staff time allows.

2. Research or class interests must be stated when scheduling an appointment. Where possible, objects of interest will be available in the laboratory upon the visitor's arrival. Access to some items may be restricted due to the object's condition, other research or museum needs, or circumstances defined by staff. Access may also be restricted for sensitive or otherwise private material.

3. In collection areas, classes or groups may not exceed ten people at any one time, and must be accompanied by Museum personnel at all times. At the Collection Manager's discretion, smaller groups may be required to insure the safety and security of the collections and visitors.

Archaeology Research Request Form, Page 1
Rev. 1/2001

4. The Archaeology Section has closed storage. Objects in the Archives, Library, or Collections may not be removed or replaced without staff authorization. Visitors, students, staff, researchers, faculty, and others, may not borrow Division objects except in cases where formal loan arrangements have been made (cf. Loan Policy).

5. Photography and photocopy work must be cleared with the Collections Manager in advance. Publication or reproduction permission for all Library, Archival, or collection materials must be obtained through separate written authorization (cf. Photo and Reproduction Policy). The visitor will be held responsible for any violations of Museum policies or statutes regarding copyright and public use.

6. No smoking, eating, or drinking is allowed in the collections at any time. Children are allowed only when accompanied by an adult and when permission has been obtained in advance. Pets are not allowed. Bags and parcels are subject to inspection. Visitors must abide by any and all requests by staff members during their visit.

7. Only pencil may be used in the work area. Objects being studied should be handled as little as possible, and should be left in their containers unless permission to remove them is granted by the Collections Manager or Curator. Appropriate gloves are required for the handling of all objects.

8. The Museum requires a citation in any published work based upon or utilizing the results of research conducted in the Museum collections. The Museum requires a copy of resulting research, published or unpublished, upon completion.

9. Slides and educational resource kits are available for public use outside the Museum. Interested persons should contact the Manager of Education Programs at (206) 685-7154.

10. For research on burial objects and related information, or objects that may be culturally sensitive, the Museum requires that the researcher contact the culturally-affiliated entities.

11. For records containing information exempt from disclosure under the Public Records Act (RCW 42.17.250; RCW 42.17.310(1)(k)), the Burke Museum will withhold such information when such release would result in the loss or damage to the resource. The Researcher's Signature below constitutes agreement with the Burke Museum that any records containing exempt information that are obtained by the Researcher from the Burke Museum will remain protected from public disclosure.

I affirm that the information provided on this form is correct. I agree to pay fees as invoiced for any reproduction or duplication of research material. I have read and agree to abide by the Conditions of Access/Code of Conduct if my request is approved. I understand that if I do not abide by these requirements, I may be asked to leave the Museum. I agree to be responsible for any damage to the collections occurring as a result of my research activities.

Researcher's Signature_____   Date_____

_____

For official use only

Materials researched

THE BURKE MUSEUM OF NATURAL HISTORY AND CULTURE

On-Campus Loan Agreement
Burke Museum of Natural History and Culture,
University of Washington, Box 353010, Seattle, WA 98195-3010

BORROWER (must be UW Faculty): Dr. Angela Close

STUDENT RESEARCHER: Amy Jordan

REASON FOR LOAN: Lithic Analysis

TEMPORARY LOCATION: Denny Hall, Room 115, Locked Cabinet supplied by Burke Archaeology Dept.

LOAN DATES: From: 10/19/2006   To: 12/8/2005

LIST OF LOAN OBJECT(S):

			IN	*HOUSING*	*OUT*
ACCN. NO.	*CATALOG NO.*	*DESCRIPTION*		*Indicate BAG or BOX*	
INITIALS/DATE	*INITIALS/DATE*				

All Lithics from East Timor UW Field School 2005, Site: IRA ARA

See attached list of bags

CREDIT: Objects must be cited with full credit as follows: East Timor UW Field School 2005, IRA ARA, catalog number ___, Material currently located at the Burke Museum of Natural History and Culture.

**SPECIAL
CONDITIONS:** Please use attached template for analysis sheets. See also attached list of Special Conditions.

LOAN APPROVED BY: _____
                        CURATOR'S SIGNATURE   DATE

LOAN PREPARED BY: _____
                        ARCHAEOLOGY COLLECTIONS STAFF   DATE

The undersigned assumes full responsibility for the object(s) listed above, subject to the conditions listed above and printed on the back of this On-campus Loan Agreement form until their return to the Burke Archaeology Dept.

_____   _____   _____   _____
BORROWER'S SIGNATURE   DATE   STUDENT RESEARCHER'S SIGNATURE   DATE

RELEASED TO STUDENT RESEARCHER BY:

_____   _____
ARCHAEOLOGY COLLECTIONS Staff   DATE

Borrower hereby acknowledges receipt from the Division of the object(s) listed above.

_____   _____
STUDENT RESEARCHER'S SIGNATURE   DATE

RECEIVED AT BURKE ARCHAEOLOGY DEPT:

_____   _____
ARCHAEOLOGY COLLECTIONS STAFF   DATE

Remarks on condition on date of return:

106   San Juan Island National Historical Park Museum Management Plan

On-Campus Loan Agreement
CONDITIONS

The Borrower and Student Researcher accept possession of the object(s) listed on the attachment for this On-Campus Loan Agreement subject to the following conditions:

CARE AND PROTECTION

1. Object(s) borrowed shall be given special care at all times to insure against loss, damage or deterioration. Object(s) must be maintained in a building equipped to protect object(s) from fire, smoke or flood damage; under 24-hour physical and/or electronic security and protected from extreme temperatures and humidity, excessive light, and from insects, vermin, dirt, or other environmental hazards. Object(s) must be handled only by designated personnel and be secured from damage and theft by appropriate locking rooms and/or cabinets.

2. Borrower and Student Researcher agree to meet the special conditions as noted on the face of the agreement. Borrower and Student Researcher must notify Burke Archaeology Department immediately, followed by a written report, including photographs, if damage or loss is discovered.

3. Objects must remain in the condition received. No cleaning, repairing, retouching, conservation, sewing or taping will be done without prior approval from the Archaeology Collections Managers or Curator. No tags or numbers will be removed from objects. No object may be altered, cleaned or repaired without permission from the Burke Archaeology Department. No pins, nails, tape, glue, wax or other materials will be used to mount objects for exhibition purposes, unless approved by the Archaeology Collections Managers or Curator in advance. When in doubt, contact the Archaeology Collections Managers.

4. All objects that are loaned must be returned with the same housing materials in which they arrived, unless otherwise directed by Archaeology Collections Managers. Housing materials will be treated in the same manner and with the same care as all other loaned objects.

5. Borrower and Student Researcher agree to comply with all labeling and rehousing requirements noted under Special Conditions.

CANCELLATION/RETURN/EXTENSION

1. Object(s) borrowed must be returned to the Burke Museum in satisfactory condition by the stated termination date.
2. If the conditions above and on the front side of this loan agreement are not followed, the Burke Archaeology Department has the right to recall the loan on short notice. Furthermore, the Burke Archaeology Department reserves the right to cancel this loan for good cause at any time, and will make every effort to give reasonable notice thereof.

Outgoing Loan Agreement

Burke Museum of Natural History and Culture, University of Washington, Box 353010,
Seattle, WA 98195-3010
Phone: 206-685-9948   Fax: 206-685-3039   Email: burkereg@u.washington.edu

Borrower: <Institution Name>   **Contact:**   <Name>
<Address>   <Address>
<Address>   <Address>
<City, State, Zip…>   <City, State, Zip…>
<Phone><Fax>   <Phone><Fax>
<Email>   <Email>

Loan   **Installation**
Dates: From: <Date>   To: <Date>   **Dates:**   From: <Date>   To: <Date>

Purpose of Loan: [ ] Exhibit   [ ] Research   [ ] Other (specify)
_____

List of Loan Object(s):
Accession No.   *Description*   *Value*

_____

Insurance: *Please read conditions on reverse. Insurance valuation in U.S. dollars:*
[ ] To be carried by Borrower
Estimated cost of the insurance premium: $_____

[ ] To be carried by the Burke Museum of Natural History and Culture
$_____

[ ] Insurance waived

Credit: If any object is labeled for display or publication, it will be credited as "Burke Museum of Natural History and Culture, Seattle".

Publications: *Please read Reproduction/Credit conditions on reverse.*

**Special
Conditions:**

**Loan
Approved By:**   _____   _____
                   Curator's Signature   Date

**Loan
Prepared By:**   _____   _____   _____
                   Museum Representative's Signature   Title   Date

_____

The Borrower hereby acknowledges receipt from the Burke Museum of Natural History and Culture of the object(s) listed above. The undersigned assumes full responsibility for the object(s) subject to the conditions printed on the back of this Outgoing Loan Agreement form until they return to the Burke Museum of Natural History and Culture.

_____   _____   _____
Borrower's Signature   Title   Date

For Office Use Only
Date returned to the BMNHC:
Received by:

Remarks on condition on date of return:

Outgoing Loan Agreement
CONDITIONS

The Borrower accepts possession of the object(s) listed on the reverse side of this Outgoing Loan Agreement subject to the following conditions:

CARE AND PROTECTION

1. Object(s) borrowed shall be given special care at all times to insure against loss, damage or deterioration. Object(s) must be maintained in a building equipped to protect object(s) from fire, smoke or flood damage; under 24-hour physical and/or electronic security and protected from extreme temperatures and humidity, excessive light, and from insects, vermin, dirt, or other environmental hazards. Object(s) must be handled only by experienced personnel and be secured from damage and theft by appropriate brackets, railings, display cases, or other responsible means.

2. The Borrower agrees to meet the special conditions as noted on the face of the agreement. Furthermore, the Burke Museum of Natural History and Culture (BMNHC) may require an inspection or approval of the actual installation by a member of its staff as a condition of the loan at the expense of the Borrower. Upon receipt and prior to return of the object(s), the Borrower must make a written record of condition. The BMNHC must be notified immediately, followed by a written report, including photographs, if damage or loss is discovered.

3. No object may be altered, cleaned or repaired without written permission from the BMNHC.

PACKING AND TRANSPORTATION

1. The object(s) will be securely packed in accordance with museum standards by experienced personnel under competent supervision.

2. The object(s) will be returned packed by experienced personnel in the same or similar materials as received unless otherwise authorized by BMNHC.

3. Costs of transportation and packing will be borne by the Borrower.

INSURANCE

1. The object(s) shall be insured during the period of this loan for the value stated on the face of this agreement under an "all-risk" wall-to-wall policy.

2. Unless otherwise agreed upon in advance, the Borrower is responsible for insuring the object(s) and providing the BMNHC with a Certificate of Insurance or a copy of the policy made out in favor to the BMNHC as an additional insured or waving rights of subrogation prior to shipment of the object(s). The BMNHC must be notified in writing at least 20 days prior to any cancellation or meaningful change in the Borrower's .policy. If the Borrower fails to provide said certificate of insurance, this failure shall constitute a waiver of insurance by the Borrower. The BMNHC shall not be responsible for any error or deficiency in information furnished by the Borrower to the insurer or for any lapses in such coverage.

3. If insured by the BMNHC under its "all-risk" wall-to-wall policy through the University of Washington Equipment Insurance Program it will be subject to the following standard exclusions: wear and tear, gradual deterioration, insects, vermin or inherent vice; repairing, restoration or retouching process; hostile or warlike action, insurrection, rebellion; nuclear reaction, or radioactive contamination.

4. If insurance is waived, the Borrower agrees to indemnify the BMNHC for any and all loss or damage to the object(s) occurring during the course of the loan, except for loss or damage resulting from wear and tear, gradual deterioration, inherent vice, war and nuclear risk.

REPRODUCTION/CREDIT

1. Photographs of object(s) may be reproduced only for exhibit catalog and publicity associated with the exhibit. All other photography requires written permission from the Burke Museum.

2. A complimentary copy of any publication or catalog illustrating object(s) from the collections of the Burke Museum must be sent to the Burke Museum.

CANCELLATION/RETURN/EXTENSION

1. Object(s) borrowed must be returned to the BMNHC in satisfactory condition by the stated termination date.

2. Any requests for extension of the loan period must be received in writing at least 20 working days prior to the expiration date of the loan.

3. If deemed necessary, the BMNHC has the right to recall a loan on short notice. Furthermore, the BMNHC reserves the right to cancel this loan for good cause at any time, and will make every effort to give reasonable notice thereof.

Outgoing Research Loan Agreement

Burke Museum of Natural History and Culture, University of Washington, Box 353010,
Seattle, WA 98195-3010
Phone: 206-685-3849   Fax: 206-685-3039   Email: lphill@u.washington.edu

Borrower:

**Loan
Dates:**   From: To:

Purpose of Loan: [X] Research [ ] Other (specify)

List of Loan Object(s):
ACCN. NO.   CATALOG NO. DESCRIPTION

Insurance: **[X] Insurance waived**

Credit: If any information about this object is displayed or published, it will be credited as "   "

Publications: Please read Reproduction/Credit conditions on reverse.

**Special
Conditions:**   **See Attached**

Loan Approved By: _____   _____
                               Curator's Signature   Date

Loan Prepared By: _____   _____
                               Museum Representative's Signature   Title   Date

The Borrower hereby acknowledges receipt from the Burke Museum of Natural History and Culture of the object(s) listed above. The undersigned assumes full responsibility for the object(s) subject to the conditions printed on the back of this Outgoing Loan Agreement form until they return to the Burke Museum of Natural History and Culture.

_____
Borrower's Signature   Title   Date

RECEIVED AT BURKE ARCHAEOLOGY DEPT:

_____   _____
ARCHAEOLOGY COLLECTIONS Staff   DATE

Remarks on condition on date of return:

Outgoing Research Loan Agreement
CONDITIONS

The Borrower accepts possession of the object(s) listed on the reverse side of this Outgoing Research Loan Agreement subject to the following conditions:

CARE AND PROTECTION

1. Object(s) borrowed shall be given special care at all times to insure against loss, damage or deterioration. Object(s) must be maintained in a building equipped to protect object(s) from fire, smoke or flood damage; under 24-hour physical and/or electronic security and protected from extreme temperatures and humidity, excessive light, and from insects, vermin, dirt, or other environmental hazards. Object(s) must be handled only by designated personnel and be secured from damage and theft by appropriate locking rooms and/or cabinets.
2. Borrower agrees to meet the special conditions as noted on the face of the agreement. Borrower must notify Burke Archaeology Department immediately, followed by a written report, including photographs, if damage or loss is discovered.
3. Objects must remain in the condition received. No cleaning, repairing, retouching, conservation, sewing or taping will be done without prior approval from the Archaeology Collections Managers or Curator. No tags or numbers will be removed from objects. No object may be altered, cleaned or repaired without permission from the Burke Archaeology Department. No pins, nails, tape, glue, wax or other materials will be used to mount objects for exhibition purposes, unless approved by the Archaeology Collections Managers or Curator in advance. When in doubt, contact the Archaeology Collections Managers.
4. All objects that are loaned must be returned with the same housing materials in which they arrived, unless otherwise directed by Archaeology Collections Managers. Housing materials will be treated in the same manner and with the same care as all other loaned objects.
5. Borrower agrees to comply with all labeling and rehousing requirements noted under Special Conditions.

REPRODUCTION/CREDIT

1. All photography requires written permission from the Burke Museum.
2. A complimentary copy of any publication discussing or illustrating object(s) from the collections of the Burke Museum must be sent to the Burke Museum.

CANCELLATION/RETURN/EXTENSION

1. Object(s) borrowed must be returned to the Burke Museum in satisfactory condition by the stated termination date.
2. If the conditions above and on the front side of this loan agreement are not followed, the Burke Archaeology Department has the right to recall the loan on short notice. Furthermore, the Burke Archaeology Department reserves the right to cancel this loan for good cause at any time, and will make every effort to give reasonable notice thereof.

Invoice of Specimens

Burke Museum of Natural History and Culture
University of Washington, Seattle, WA 98195-3010

Fr: Mary Collins, Director
Museum of Anthropology
Washington State University
Pullman, WA 99164-4910

To: Burke Museum
Archaeology Department
University of Washington
Box 353010
Seattle, WA 98195

How Shipped: Hand delivered

Shipping Date: April 8, 2009

The Material described below has been accepted as:

__X__ Transfer of custody

___ Return of identified material

___ Return of material borrowed from us
___ Return of material borrowed by us

___ Return of material
___ Other

---

42 boxes of archaeological material and maps from the Martin Site (45-PC-7).

This material is being transferred from WSU to be reunited with other archaeological collections already stored at the Burke from the same site.

Released By: Mary Collins, WSU _____ _____ Date: _____

Received By: Megon Noble, Burke Museum_____ Date: _____

Received in Good Condition, Except as Noted:

1. The Burke Museum retains the sole copyright for its holdings and all images depicting its holdings. Photographic images that are in the care of, or are the property of, the Burke Museum, or photographs, photocopies, or artistic renderings of collection items that are in the care of, or are the property of, the Burke Museum, shall not be reproduced, resold, or commercially used without the specific written permission of the Burke Museum. In some cases the Museum does not hold literary or other copyrights to some items and it is the user's responsibility to secure those rights where necessary.

2. Permission for reproduction is granted for one publication, one edition, and one language only, unless specified. Requests for reproduction must be submitted on the Reproduction Permission form. Additional language editions and revised new editions will be considered upon application. All images must be returned to the Burke Museum after use.

3 No images may be used to show or imply that the Burke Museum endorses any commercial product or enterprise, or concurs with the opinions expressed in, or the accuracy of, any text used with the images. The Museum may refuse permission to reproduce images if the reproduction does not meet Museum standards, if the reproductions are used in ways which conflict with the purposes of the Museum, or if their use would be detrimental to specimens or to the reputation of the Museum.

4. Commercial use of artifacts will incur a minimum fee of $150 per BW and $350 per color image from color slides for one-time use, to be negotiated based upon the nature of the commercial use. An additional $100.00 per image is charged for photographs from 4x5 color transparencies. Rental fees for transparencies are $100 for 3 months. Images photographed from existing publications will incur a minimum fee of $75.00 per BW and $200.00 per color. Use fees for digital productions, including WEB use, are based on the resolution: $200 for low resolution digital scan (72 dpi) and $350 for high resolution digital scan (300dpi) images. The digital scan must be destroyed after use. Charges for commercial use of BW historical images will incur a fee of $75 for one-time use. A $10 handling fee is charged for reproduction of photographs in scholarly, museum, or non-profit publications; all other use fees are waived for those with 501(C)(3) status. Permission to publish is contingent upon receipt of the appropriate fees and a signed Reproduction Request form.

5. All reproduced images must be given a credit line, preferably at the picture's edge. In the case of filmstrips or videotapes, credit may be listed in any accompanying brochure and/or in the film's credits. Unless otherwise specified, please credit: Courtesy of the Burke Museum of Natural History and Culture, catalog # _____

6. As part of the agreement to grant reproduction permission, the Burke Museum requires that, immediately upon publication, one copy of the publication (book, audio or videotape, film, commercial presentation, etc.) be furnished at no cost to the Burke Museum for use in the divisional library. Further, two copies of any image photographed by the user must be furnished to the appropriate Museum division at no cost.

7. For photos of burial objects and related information, or objects that may be culturally sensitive, the Museum requires that the requested contact the culturally-affiliated entities.

Revised 3/2004

Field Collection Form (Collected material not associated with survey, inventory, or monitoring)

Date:	Collected by:		
	Address:	Tel:	
		E-Mail:	
UTM	Zone:	Northing:	Easting:
Location description (directions for relocating the site):			
Justification for collecting:			
Description of object:			
Were there other similar materials in the same area but not collected?	Yes	No	
Were photographs taken of the area? (If so, Please attach)	Yes	No	
Signature of collector:			
Signature of park employee receiving the object: